WILDFLOWERS
of the BWCA and
the NORTH
SHORE

Written by
MARK
SPARKY
STENSAAS

Illustrated by
RICK
KOLLATH

Kollath+Stensaas Publishing
394 Lake Avenue South, Suite 406
Duluth, MN 55802
218.727.1731
kollath@cpinternet.com

WILDFLOWERS *of the* BWCA *and the* NORTH SHORE

Printed in the United States of America.
10 9 8 7 6 5 4 3 2 1 First Edition

ISBN 0-9673793-3-4

To Mom and Dad,
who have always supported me
in whatever crazy endeavor
I've taken up.
    —Mark Sparky Stensaas

To my father, Al Kollath, with
gratitude, for infecting me
with his love of the outdoors,
and much besides.

    —Rick Kollath

CONTENTS

ACKNOWLEDGEMENTS

"Botany" is not quite my middle name, but many folks have been willing to share bits of their vast knowledge with me and instill a love of North Woods flora. My plant ecology and botany professors at the University of Minnesota—Duluth, Dr. Paul "Doc" Monson and Dr. David Schimpf, went to great lengths to give us students a "green" experience when spring in Duluth does not often come until the week after finals. Gary Walton, who may be one of the best field botanists in Minnesota, has willingly shared many of his favorite haunts with me. He has aided in many of my identification conundrums and taught me proper field collection techniques. Hikes with naturalists who know more about a topic than you do are always inspiring. Thanks to Mary Shedd, Cal Harth, Bunter Knowles, Ken Gilbertson, Larry Weber and Cindy Johnson-Groh. I have picked the brains of wildflower wizards Chel Anderson, Deb Shubat, Molly and Ken Hoffman, Deb Pomroy-Petry and the late Quetico and Sleeping Giant Provincial Park naturalist, Shan Walshe. Thanks to all!

Mark Sparky Stensaas

Reviewers make all the difference in the world when you want your book to be readable. Thanks to Catherine Long, Jane Reed, Connie Stensaas and Tim Conklin for keeping us honest and in check.

Rick Kollath, Mark Sparky Stensaas
Duluth, Minnesota
May 1, 2003

INTRODUCTION

Welcome to the wonderful world of wildflowers. "Flower peeking" (not to be confused with flower picking) is an addicting hobby that can be practiced for a little over half the year in the North Woods. That's not bad.

We chose flowers that were diagnostic of their habitat and either very common, very interesting or very unique. My apologies if we left out your favorite.

Organization by Habitat

The 108 species included in this book are grouped by their preferred habitat. If you are standing on a floating bog then you can most likely find the flowers that surround you in the *Northern Bogs* chapter of the book. Most chapters are broken down further by subchapters. Under *Northern Bogs* we have separated species into *Carnivores of the Floating Bog, Sphagnum Moss Mats* and *Black Spruce Bogs*.

Descriptionless Text

We have purposely left out most physical descriptions of the plant and let Rick's wonderful illustrations do the talking. I don't have to write "fuzzy stem" if you can see it in the illustration. We leave the technical descriptions including stamen, sepal and pistil count to the botany reference books.

Natural History *ad Nauseam*

We had to fill all that white space left vacant between illustrations by the lack of technical plant descriptions (Did you know botanists have 27 terms for "fuzzy?"), so we threw in gobs of natural history instead. It's more interesting anyway. You'll find lots of native American uses, old and new herbal remedies, colorful common names, Greek and Latin etymological origins, gleaned gems of hardcore scientific research and plenty of quotes from Henry David Thoreau's journals.

Size Matters

Next to each species is a height icon that gives an average range of mature plant heights. For some species such as the water-lilies, we have shown the length of the leaf and for aquatic emergents it is the height above the water that we give.

Phenology Phun

Phenograms are placed next to each species. The violet bar represents the main flower-

May	June	July

ing period for that species. Use this as a guide to know when to go searching for a species. For example, you'd know by looking at the phenogram not to look for Yellow Trout Lily, a spring ephemeral, in August.

Checklists are Us

Every book we put out has to have a checklist. We have included one in the back of the book.

We hope you enjoy *Wildflowers of the Boundary Waters and North Shore* and take it with you on every hike.

TIPS FOR FLOWER PEEKERS

1. Get a Loupe
For a closeup look at tiny flower heads or to count stamens and pistil parts, use a hand lens or loupe. Quality 10-power loupes are usually available at university bookstores or gem and rock shops.

2. Learn the Floral Formula
If a flower has 6 petals, 3 sepals, 6 stamens and a 1-parted pistil, the formula would be written "6p3s6st1pi." It forces you to closely examine each flower and will result in easier identifications as most families have a unique floral formula. Learn the "floral formula" and use it.

3. Sketch Pads are Handy
Small sketch pads are great for taking field notes and drawing unknown flowers. You can reference your notes and sketches at home when identifying the flower with your home-bound reference books.

4. Go Digital!
The new breed of compact digital cameras focus extremely close. Some even have a swivel LCD viewfinder so you can easily take ground-level shots. Use this 21st-century tool to document your botanical finds.

5. Wear Grubby Pants
Flower peeking involves getting down on your hands and knees to get that really good look. Wear grubby pants or, if it is very wet, rain pants.

6. Bring along this Field Guide
It may also be "worth the weight" to bring along a more comprehensive guide. Some of our favorites for the North Woods include: *Peterson's Field Guide to Flowers*, *Newcomb's Wildflower Guide* and *What's Doin' the Bloomin'* by Duluthians Clayton and Michele Oslund. If you are going on a spring walk and are familiar with floral keys, consider *Spring Flora of Minnesota* by Thomas Morley. Be warned, it has no photos or illustrations—only text and family keys.

7. Pick only when Appropriate
Picking flowers in state parks, national parks, scientific and natural areas and on The Nature Conservancy land is prohibited, but if you are in a remote location that permits it and run across a mystery flower where there are more than ten present, pick it and place it in a portable flower press.

8. Make a Flower Press
A simple press can be made with two 4-inch by 6-inch pieces of 3/4-inch plywood. Sandwich the specimen between two sheets of acid-free blotting paper that are between two pieces of corrugated cardboard. Make sure the flower parts all show before cranking down the screws. Strap or tie the plywood covers. When you get home place the mini-press under a pile of heavy books for a week. You could also use bolts and wingnuts to secure the press.

9. Prepare for Off-Trail
Bushwacking to find far-flung flora requires some careful planning. Pack a compass (know how to use it), map, strike-anywhere matches in a waterproof case, knife, whistle, water and energy bar. A GPS unit can be handy for finding your way and recording flower locations (lock in the coordinates of the trailhead or your car before hiking). Clear glasses or lightly tinted sunglasses will protect your eyes from getting poked by rogue branches while wandering off trail.

NORTHERN HARDWOOD FOREST
Spring Ephemerals

An old growth northern hardwood forest is dominated by Sugar Maple, Basswood and Red Oak with a smattering of Yellow Birch and a few scattered large White Pine and White Spruce. Hemlock and Beech join the mix farther east in northern Wisconsin and the Upper Peninsula of Michigan. The maple-basswood forest is especially vibrant when the spring wildflowers are in bloom during late April and May. You can find northern hardwood forests on the highlands above Lake Superior's North Shore (Sugar Maple dominated) and in pocket stands from central Minnesota east across the U.P. of Michigan.

Here Today, Gone Tomorrow
Ephemerals are spring woodland wildflowers that bloom before the leaves fully develop on the overarching trees; all their vegetative parts disappear by summer when the canopy closes. This survival strategy allows them to utilize the abundant sunlight shining down through the bare tree branches to reach the forest floor. It's a good thing, too, as mid-summer in a hardwood forest is a very dark place indeed...no place for a sun-loving plant.

Ephemerals are generalists when it comes to pollinators. A single bee or fly can fertilize a flower by simply walking around on it.

Spring: Ephemeral flowers bloom. Most have white blossoms that are pollinated by early insects such as flies and bumblebees.

Late Spring: Leaves of the canopy trees unfurl, shading out the forest floor. Leaves of the ephemerals begin to wither from the tip down to the base. Nutrients are gradually reabsorbed into the underground corm.

Summer: Our ephemerals have basically disappeared from sight and moved underground. In the corm, starches decrease and are converted to soluble sugars to make more available energy for greater frost resistance and to fuel next spring's growth.

Early Fall: New roots begin to develop.

Winter: Shoots elongate as the plant gets ready to break the surface in spring.

Early Spring: As the snow melts and the ground warms up, the stored sugars kick in causing a growth spurt. Leaves push through the dirt, and flower buds develop.

Wood Anemone
Anemone quinquefolia

These guys make a very early appearance in the spring woodlands. Their leaves are dark green, not a bright springy green. Wood Anemones open during sunny spring days allowing early-season insects (bees and beelike flies) to pollinate them. On cloudy, cool days the flowers close up and droop thereby saving their precious pollen for the insects. This cool weather position is probably responsible for several common names including granny's nightcap, bowbells and drops-of-snow.

Adonis, Aphrodite or Venus?

Anemone is thought to be a corruption of the Semitic name for Adonis — *Namaan*. There is some confusion as to whether the first anemones arose from the soil where Adonis' blood was spilled or from Aphrodite's tears as she mourned for the slain Adonis. Some even ascertain that it was Venus' tears, not Aphrodite's, that started it all.

This line from a poem is not specific enough to clear up the mystery, "And where a tear has dropped a windflower blows." Your guess is as good as mine.

The Lilies of the Field?

"Consider the lilies of the field, how they grow; they toil not, neither do they spin: And yet I say unto you, that even Solomon in all his glory was not arrayed like one of these."
    Matthew 6:28-29.

Michael Zohary, author of *Plants of the Bible*, believes that the "lilies" referred to in this passage are Crown Anemones which he says "in early spring…dot every field, bush, wasteland and sandy hill in all the Mediteranean."

Ill Wind

To the Persians, a wind that passed over a field of anemones was poisoned. Because of this they adopted the anemone as a symbol of illness. "Death flower" was the name given to the anemone by the Chinese who planted it on graves. No such ill fortune is attributed to our Wood Anemone.

Flowery Prose

"Delicate blossom… holds the very essence of spring and purity in its quivering cup."

So goes the description of Wood Anemone by an admirer. Those early naturalists sure were a flowery bunch.

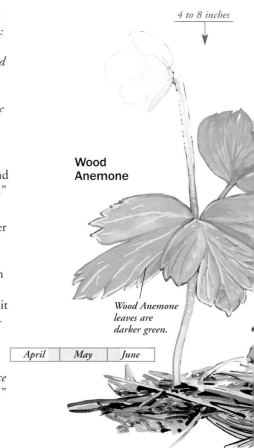

4 to 8 inches

Wood Anemone

Wood Anemone leaves are darker green.

| April | May | June |

Spring Beauty & Carolina Spring Beauty
Claytonia virginica & Claytonia caroliniana (not illustrated)

Spring Beauty

4 to 6 inches

In older northern hardwood forests, Spring Beauty grows in profusion, blanketing the ground in places. Carolina Spring Beauty has wider leaves than its close cousin and is more common in the highland forests of Minnesota's North Shore.

Though a flower can hardly have a more fitting name than "Spring Beauty," others have tried; fairy spuds, good-morning-spring, grass-flower and Mayflower are all old colloquial names. "Mayflower" has been attached to several flowers of spring including False Lily-of-the-Valley, Round-lobed Hepatica and Wood Anemone.

April	May	June

Longfellow's Beauty of the Spring
Longfellow's *The Song of Hiawatha*, makes reference to Spring Beauty. The youth Segwun has seen the icy face of winter melt away, and now…

"On the hearth-stone of the wigwam
Where the fire had smoked and smoldered,
Saw the earliest flower of Spring-time,
Saw the Beauty of the Spring-time,
Saw the Miskodeed in blossom."

X-Ray Vision
Spring Beauty may be capable of detecting lengthening days (photoperiod) beneath the snow and communicate with its underground plant parts. Research has shown that Spring Beauty is able to grow leaves and floral parts before emerging from the soil.

Flower-friendly Forest Fungi

It is now understood that 95 percent of all land plants belong to genera that form associations with soil fungi. Since the German forest pathologist, A. B. Frank, first described a tree-fungus relationship in 1885, our knowledge of mycorrhizae (white, multi-branched roots of a fungus) has come slowly. Most are familiar with the dependency of orchids, heaths and Indian Pipe on soil fungi for nutrition, but even our spring ephemerals of the northern hardwood forest need their fungal buddies.

It's a two-way street. Mycorrhizae invade the plant roots, greatly increasing the surface area available for absorption of water and nutrients. The fortunate fungus receives plant-produced carbon and the lucky flower has a direct pipeline to fungal-gathered nutrients like phosphorous, zinc and copper. This underground relationship is a win-win deal.

Round-lobed Hepatica
Hepatica americana

One of our earliest spring wildflowers, often blooms amid patches of melting snow. Hepatica flowers actually have no petals. What looks like petals are really sepals and can be white, pink or purplish.

Other common names for this plant include blunt-lobed hepatica, liverleaf, three-leaved liverwort, blue anemone, livermoss, herb trinity and squirrel-cup.

Doctrine of Signatures

This doctrine held that a plant could cure the body part it resembled. Following this line of thinking, early healers thought that hepatica leaves resembled the human liver and that it aided in "stirring a torpid liver." That is how hepatica got its name; *hepatitis* is Greek for "liver." Rycharde Banckes, a very early herbalist in England, wrote in 1525, "This herbe is called Lyverworte. His vertue is to destroy and clense the hardness of the lyver." Liverwort, or hepatica, became all the medicinal rage in the 1880s. In fact, in 1883, American pickers could not gather enough to meet demand, so over 425,000 pounds were imported from Germany.

Hillbilly Love Charm
Folklorist James Mooney, writing about Carolina mountain folk in the

3 to 5 inches

Flowers may be white, pink or blue.

Spring Beau[t] may bloom amongst pa[t] of melting s[now]

Note the pubescent (fuzzy) stems.

| April | May | June |

1880s, related the belief that a girl could get her man by "secretly throwing over his clothing some of the powder made by rubbing together a few heart leaves which have been dried by the fire."

Some native peoples used hepatica as a charm to bring them good fortune when trapping animals.

Dwarf Ginseng
Panax trifolium

This is NOT the valuable, Chinese wonder-drug type of ginseng, so don't even think about going out and digging up this early-blooming plant. Dwarf Ginseng grows from a small globby root called a corm. The tiniest of plants only produce a whorl of leaves (no flowers). Medium-sized plants not only produce a whorl of leaves but a small umbel of tiny white, all-male flowers —all stamens and no pistil. The largest plants are hermaphroditic with both male (stamens) and female (pistil) parts.

Sex-changing Plant

Individual plants can change from male (flowers with only stamens) to hermaphrodite (flowers with both male and female parts) and back again several times over several seasons. Males produce two to three times more flowers per plant than the larger hermaphrodites and 1.2 times more pollen per flower. Hermaphrodites seem to be functionally female. The male flower's stamens present pollen for a longer time and more in timing with stigma presentation than the stamens on hermaphrodites.

Small solitary bees that are active in spring pollinate Dwarf Ginseng. Competition between the male plants seems to be the reason for the increased production of pollen and more exact timing. This would also help insure cross-pollination and a better genetic mix for Dwarf Ginseng.

3 to 6 inches

| April | May | June |

White Trout Lily & Yellow Trout Lily
Erythronium albidum (White) & Erythronium americanum (Yellow)

Trout lilies are plants worth seeking out in the mad rush of early-spring-blooming flowers. Look for them in the most pristine remnants of northern hardwood forest. They seem to prefer the company of Black Ash and wetter soils.

Some still call these two dogtooth-violets but it is such a misleading name; they are not violets. Of course, neither are they trout, but the spotted leaves do somewhat resemble the markings of a Brook Trout. Other names for trout lilies from America's past include amberbell, adder's-tongue, adderleaf, common fawn-lily, jonquil, lamb's-tongue, lillette, deer's-tongue, rattlesnake-violet, star-strikers, trout flower, serpent's-tongue, wild yellow-lily, yellow bells, yellow-hookers, and yellow snowdrop. The best common name of all came from John Josselyn in 1672, who called it yellow bastard daffodil.

4 to 10 inches

Spotted leaves remind some of trout markings.

Flower of White Trout Lily.

Yellow Trout Lily

John Burroughs's Wisdom
Early American naturalist John Burroughs speculated on the common names for these lilies in his 1894 book, *Riverby*, "How it came to be called 'adder's tongue' I do not know, probably from the spotted character of the leaf, which might suggest a snake, though it in no wise resembles a snake's tongue. A fawn is spotted too, and 'fawn lily' would be better than adder's tongue. Still better is the name 'trout lily' which has been recently proposed. It blooms along the trout streams, and its leaf is as mottled as a trout's back."

Native Contraception
Iroquois girls ate parts of the raw plant to keep from getting pregnant.

April	May	June

Bloodroot
Sanguinaria canadensis

Bloodroot is one of our earliest spring flowers. But Bloodroot, more than other ephemerals, enjoys open areas that are free of canopy trees. Let the sun shine down! The flower petals spread wide in full sun but stay huddled together on cloudy days and at night. Why? Possibly to save pollen for pollen-gathering insects that are active only on sunny days. The leaf arises from the ground and wraps around the stem as if the plant is wearing a shawl. The leaf will continue to grow, getting quite large and spreading wide. Well after the flower dies away, the leaf will still be around.

Bloodroot is a second cousin to the Opium Poppy; well, at least both are in the Papaveraceae family.

Bloodroot ranges from Quebec to Florida and west to Kansas and Minnesota.

Other names for Bloodroot include Indian paint, red root, sweet slumber, tetterwort, pochoon (puccoon) and coon root.

Root of Blood
Sanguinaria translates to "bleeding." Low in the stem the sap is blood red. When rubbed on the skin, the red leaves an orange streak. The Ojibwa used the sap as face paint and as a dye for baskets and clothing.

The "blood" in Bloodroot is actually red latex found only in the root.

| March | April | May |

4 to 8 inches

Good Plant...Bad Plant
The root latex is full of potent alkaloids, similar to those of its cousin, Opium Poppy. Called sanguinarine, chelerythrine, protopine and homochelidonine, these alkaloids are toxic in large doses and possibly not-so-large doses. Be warned. All parts of this plant are poisonous, but toxins are most concentrated in the roots after the leaves open. An overdose can be fatal. Absolutely do not use if pregnant or nursing. In India, sanguinarine-contaminated cooking oils have been linked to glaucoma, diarrhea, edema, heart disease and miscarriage.

But if prepared and used properly, the alkaloids can have positive benefits. Here's a list of uses described by modern-day herbalists: Sanguinarine has antiseptic, anesthetic and anticancer properties. It is also considered to be antibacterial, antiedemic, anti-inflammatory, antioxidant, diuretic, emetic, expectorant, fungicide, gastrocontractant, hypertensive, pesticide, respirastimulant, antiplaque, antiperiodontic, antigingivitic and more. Ringworm, warts, tumors and fungoid growths have been treated with a fluid extract. Other herbalists have used it as a rinse for eradicating dental plaque.

Current herbal products available on the internet and at health food stores include a sanguinarine-based toothpaste and mouth rinse. Berberine, also found in Bloodroot, has shown promising results in "fighting brain tumors and many other cancers" according to one website.

Historically, Native American healers across the country have used Bloodroot for respiratory disorders (asthma, bronchitis and lung disorders), laryngitis, fevers and rheumatism.

Love Charm

Ponca tribe bachelors would rub it on their palms and shake hands with the women they wanted to marry. Within a week she would succumb and say "yes." Women of the Notteway Indian tribe of the southeast United States used *pochoon* root to "improve their invisible charms."

Bloodroot leaves are around long after the flower is gone.

Wild Ginger
Asarum canadense

4 to 8 inches

Get down on your hands and knees in the early spring forest and gently scrape away last year's dead tree leaves to find the wonderful and bizarre flower of Wild Ginger. The heart-shaped leaves are easy to spot, but the stinky flower lies in the shadows of the duff, for it's here that the beetles, flies, ants and slugs that pollinate the plant live.

Native Knowledge

The Thompson and Okanagan Indians of the Pacific Northwest ground up the lemon-ginger smelling root and mixed it with Sphagnum Moss to make soft, sweet-smelling bedding for infants. Some Indian tribes used it as a female contraceptive. Indians of eastern Canada made an infusion to stabilize arrhythmias and relieve heart palpitations and heart pain.

Ginger Snaps?

Yes, the root can be dug up and used as a substitute for grocery-store-ginger. My friend Ingrid has done this with great success. Please, only pick one plant for every ten you leave intact. Of course, do not dig up any wild edibles in state parks or other protected areas.

April	May	June

Look closely! The flower is often hiding under dead leaves.

...ound-dwelling insects ...llinate Wild Ginger.

Dutchman's Breeches
Dicentra cucullaria

Once you've seen the tiny, white, billowy pants hanging upside down as if on a clothesline, its hard to call this plant anything else—but others have; butterfly-banners, kitten-breeches, little-boy's-breeches, soldier's-cap are other colorful common names.

Throwing Love

Ethnobotanist Huron Smith reported in 1923 that Dutchman's Breeches was used by the Menomini Indians as a valuable love charm. The first method described sounds anything but romantic: the suitor threw the plant at his beloved, attempting to hit her with it. The other method is also bizarre: he chewed the root and then breathed out the plant's essence hoping it would waft into his target's nostrils, making her follow him wherever he went. But who are we to judge considering our current methods of dating and mating.

5 to 9 inches

Native Sports Medicine

Iroquois runners drank a tea of Dutchman's Breeches leaves and other herbs to make their legs strong. They needed endurance for delivering messages and scouting far flung territories.

The lovely pink-and-white domestic Bleeding Heart, seen in so many gardens, is a Japanese cousin to Dutchman's Breeches. Both are of the genus Dicentra.

March	April	May

Sessile Bellwort
Uvularia sessilifolia

Meet the smaller, paler, but often more abundant cousin of Large-flowered Bellwort. The nodding flowers are a creamy yellow instead of a sun-shiny bright yellow, and the leaves clasp the stem ("sessile" means the leaves have no stalk but attach directly to the stem). Many folks know it by the name wild-oats.

Thoreau-vian Quote

Henry David Thoreau's main quest in life was to find God in nature. When he met the humble, bowing Sessile Bellwort in Concord's spring woodlands of 1852, he wrote, "The single modest-colored flower gracefully drooping, neat, with a fugacious, richly spiced fragrance, facing the ground, the dry leaves, as if unworthy to face the heavens."

Buck Magic

Ojibwa hunters believed the root of this plant to be strong medicine. It was carried as a charm to attract White-tailed deer.

Large-flowered Bellwort
Uvularia perfoliata

Large areas of the northern hardwood forest are covered by this bright yellow flower, often blooming alongside its cousin, Sessile Bellwort. Large-flowered Bellwort is a common spring ephemeral of the eastern states except at the extreme ends: Maine and Florida.

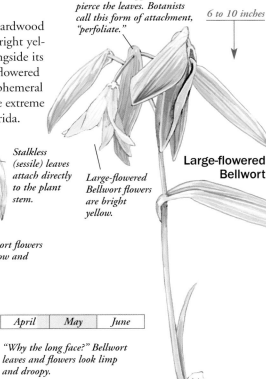

Flower stems appear to pierce the leaves. Botanists call this form of attachment, "perfoliate."

6 to 10 inches

Large-flowered Bellwort

Stalkless (sessile) leaves attach directly to the plant stem.

Large-flowered Bellwort flowers are bright yellow.

Sessile Bellwort

Sessile Bellwort flowers are pale yellow and barely open.

Young bellwort shoots make an excellent substitute for asparagus.

4 to 8 inches

April	May	June

"Why the long face?" Bellwort leaves and flowers look limp and droopy.

Don't be fooled by bellwort's droopy and wilted appearance—it always looks this way. This is a type of inflorescence known as "nodding." The leaves seem to be pierced through by the stem. *Perfoliata* is Latin for this type of attachment.

This larger of the two yellow bellworts is also called haybells, cowbells, merrybells, strawflower and, along with Sessile Bellwort, wild-oats.

Uvula-la-la-la

You know that "thing" that hangs down in the back of your throat? It's called the uvula and apparently someone thought that this plant's nodding flower resembled it, hence the genus *Uvularia*. A closely related European species is credited with starting it all. Gerarde, in 1633, wrote, "Throote wort or Uvula woort, of the vertue it hath against the pain and swelling thereof."

8 to 12 inches

| April | May | June |

Wild Leek
Allium tricoccum

Scan the forest floor of a northern hardwood forest in early spring and you will likely see several green bunches of Wild Leek leaves poking up through the dead, gray and brown leaves. To be sure you've found Wild Leek, simply crush a bit of leaf and smell the pungent odor of onions. The leeks themselves are developing underground. They are best dug up when the leaves begin to wither. I've used them to liven up chili or stews. Be careful; they are very strong.

Wild Leek "onion" dug from the dirt.

Wild Leek leaves can be a problem plant for dairy farmers. Cows who eat the leaves tend to give bitter-tasting milk.

Not only "The Windy City"

Ojibwa people knew the prairies at the south end of Lake Michigan as *she-kag-ong* or "place of the wild onion." Today we know this area as Chicago—a corruption of the original Ojibwa word.

Wild Leek flower heads appear in the summer woods long after the leaves have disappeared.

| June | July | August |

Ant Distribution Network Inc.

Seeds of trilliums have attached fat globules called elaiosomes. These tasty treats are high in fats and oils; ants love them. They crave them so strongly that they often don't wait for the seeds to mature. In an ant-frenzy, they cut a hole in the unripe fruit to get at the fatty treats, marching them up to 70 yards back to their burrows.

Food locations are communicated to other ants by external hormones called pheromones. After the elaiosome is eaten, the intact seed is dumped in a midden (a pile of unused food parts). A few of these discarded seeds may eventually germinate thereby spreading the plants across the landscape.

Ant-dispersed plant species are called myrmecochores. Bloodroot, Dutchman's Breeches, violets, anemones, hepaticas and trilliums are in this group.

Large-flowered Trillium
Trillium grandiflorum

Meet the star attraction in the parade of spring ephemerals—Large-flowered Trillium. Acres of hardwood forest can be covered with the large white blossoms. It's almost as if a Kleenex® factory has exploded!

The genus *Trillium* has an odd worldwide-distribution. Many different species are found in North America, from the Pacific Northwest to the Rockies and east to the Atlantic coast. Other species are found across Siberia to China, Korea, Japan and down to the Himilayas. But in between, in Europe, trilliums are totally absent.

Three is the Word.
Trilliums possess three leaves, three green sepals, three petals, a three-parted pistil, three spreading stigmas and six stamens. *Trillium* is Latin for three. Large-flowered Trillium is a well-named plant.

6 to 10 inches

Trillium is all about threes: three leaves, three petals, three sepals.

April	May	June

Stinking Benjamin

Trilliums usually self-pollinate. This task is performed as stamens drop pollen on the pistil of the same plant. Self-pollination reduces genetic variation. Cross-fertilization does occur occasionally as flies attracted by the plant's smell carry pollen from one flower to another. Large-flowered Trillium only has a faint odor while its southern cousin, Stinking Benjamin (*Trillium erectum*)—like its name implies—has a strong stench.

Double Dormancy

Remember those ant-abandoned trillium seeds we talked about in the *Ant Distribution Inc.* sidebar? Before they can germinate, the seeds must endure two winters. Fueled by stored endosperm, the seed manages to sprout a tiny rhizome in its first year. During the second spring, the cotyledon emerges and breaks the surface as a one-leaved trillium baby. This stage may last for two to four years; each year the single leaf gets larger. The three-leaved adolescent stage lasts at least two

more years. Finally, a sexually-mature flowering plant graces the northern hardwood forest five to 20 years after a single ant abandoned a seed.

Yellow Jacket Express.

Yellow jackets (*Vespula* species) were found to distribute trillium seeds in the Blue Ridge Mountains of North Carolina. Attracted by the same lipid-rich elaiosomes on the seeds that ants find so delicious, the yellow jackets were seen flying off with the seeds of three species (*Trillium cuneatum*, *T. undulatum* and *T. catesbaei*).

Clemson University researchers found that yellow jackets carried the seeds an average of 1.4 meters but this distance is skewed to the low side due to the fact that many flew out of sight and the dispersal distance could not be measured. It is believed that the seeds were being carried back to the yellow jacket's

Vespula vulgaris (better known as the Common Yellow Jacket) makes off with a trillium seed. Wasps are attracted to fat globule on the seed's coat.

underground nest. The advantage in plant dispersal and survival is obvious; ants are only able to disperse seeds a short distance while yellow jackets can move seeds much farther.

This distribution phenomenon is not limited to the Southeast. Erik Jules of the University of Michigan watched five Common Yellow Jackets (*Vespula vulgaris*) take turns entering the dried seedpod of Western Trillium (*T. ovatum*) in southwestern Oregon. Each one would free a seed and fly off with it. One even paused for a little snack, taking a few bites of the seed's fatty elaiosome before flying off.

Rosy the Trillium

In a "drift" of trillium blossoms scan for the pink petals of an aging bloom. They make stunning subjects for photos. On occasion a flower opens pink instead of white and stays that color. This rare form is called *Trillium grandiflorum* forma *roseum*.

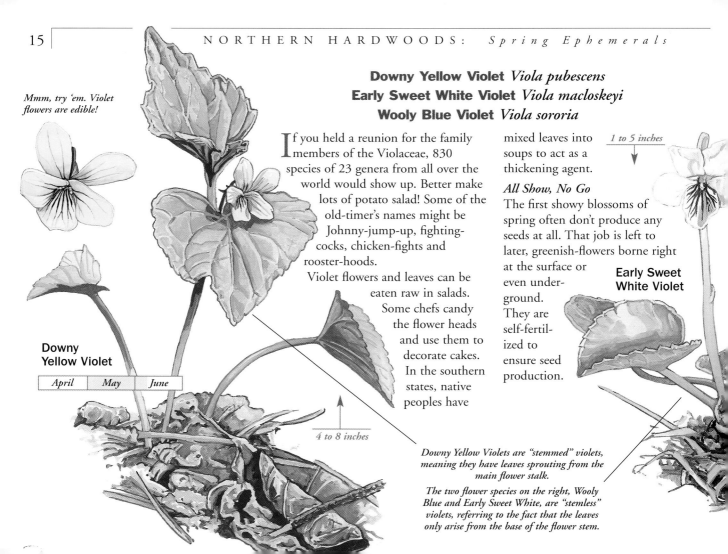

Mmm, try 'em. Violet flowers are edible!

Downy Yellow Violet *Viola pubescens*
Early Sweet White Violet *Viola macloskeyi*
Wooly Blue Violet *Viola sororia*

If you held a reunion for the family members of the Violaceae, 830 species of 23 genera from all over the world would show up. Better make lots of potato salad! Some of the old-timer's names might be Johnny-jump-up, fighting-cocks, chicken-fights and rooster-hoods.

Violet flowers and leaves can be eaten raw in salads. Some chefs candy the flower heads and use them to decorate cakes. In the southern states, native peoples have mixed leaves into soups to act as a thickening agent.

1 to 5 inches

All Show, No Go
The first showy blossoms of spring often don't produce any seeds at all. That job is left to later, greenish-flowers borne right at the surface or even under-ground. They are self-fertil-ized to ensure seed production.

Early Sweet White Violet

Downy Yellow Violet

April	May	June

4 to 8 inches

Downy Yellow Violets are "stemmed" violets, meaning they have leaves sprouting from the main flower stalk.

The two flower species on the right, Wooly Blue and Early Sweet White, are "stemless" violets, referring to the fact that the leaves only arise from the base of the flower stem.

Explosive Ejection

Some violets use an explosive seed dispersal system. Drying capsule walls contract suddenly, catapulting the seeds a fair distance.

Ant-Aided Travel

Violet seeds have attached oil bodies (elaiosomes) that ants crave. Ants carry them away to underground burrows where they eat the fat and discard the intact seed. As with Dutchman's Breeches, trilliums, hepaticas, anemones and Bloodroot, ant-aided dispersal ensures the spread of the species.

2 to 5 inches

Wooly Blue Violet

April	May	June

April	May	June

Ultraviolet Highway

We have learned that bees and some other insects can see ultraviolet light; people cannot. When an earth-dwelling human looks at a Marsh Marigold flower, we see a pretty yellow blossom.

Bees and other pollinating insects see a roadmap to the pollen and nectar—a dark blue-purple center with converging lines on colorless sepals. Early-season bees and syrphid flies are the main pollinators of this spring flower.

Marsh Marigold seen in visible light

Marsh Marigold seen in ultra-violet light

Marsh Marigold
Caltha palustris

Often the first sign of spring flora that most folks notice are "rivers" of yellow Marsh Marigold blossoms in wooded swamps. Clusters of plants grow along the wet edges of small creeks and in wooded swamps.

"Marsh Buttercup" would be a better common name for this wet-loving *Caltha* species as it is neither a marigold nor a cowslip; both are from entirely different flower families. Since it also grows in England, there's a plethora of antiquated common names: bullflower, capers, crazy-Bets, gools, drunkards, king-cup, horse-blob, Mary-buds, soldier's-buttons, palsywort, water-bowls, water-dragon and water-goggle. "Crazy-Bets" is what English children believed your fate would be if one stared at the flowers for too long.

Shakespeare's Golden Eyes

Marsh Marigolds even made it into William Shakespeare's *Cymbeline*:

> *"And winking Mary-buds begin*
> *To ope their golden eyes;*
> *With everything that pretty is,*
> *My lady sweet arise!"*

Yellow Brick Road

One author/naturalist observed that dense Marsh Marigold blossoms clustered in a stream bottom created a "yellow brick road" winding its way through the brown of an early-spring woodland.

Wart-reducer or Blister-causer?

Cultural Anthropologist Frances Densmore studied the Ojibwa in the early 20th century. She discovered that they used a mashed poultice of boiled Marsh Marigold roots to suppress coughs and heal various "owies."

Early European-settler folklore held that the caustic stem juice of this plant could reduce warts. Ironically, simply touching the leaves can cause blisters in some folks. Live plants are laced with two toxins, helleborin and protoanemonin, that can cause stomach inflammation and heart problems. Deer and moose don't mind, though, as they readily munch the swamp plants.

April	May	June

8 to 18 inches

Skunk Cabbage
Symplocarpus foetidus

Though not common in the North Woods, I couldn't resist putting this bizarre plant in the book. Look for the dappled-red, sheathing hood-like spathe (modified bract) and stubby flower-bearing spadix in the wet wooded swamps of early spring. Long after the flower disappears the leaves remain; they grow to gigantic size. Adam and Eve could have been so lucky!

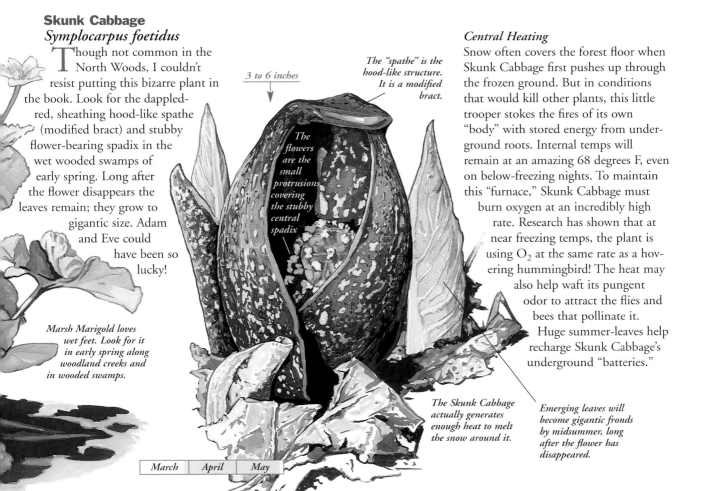

3 to 6 inches

The "spathe" is the hood-like structure. It is a modified bract.

The flowers are the small protrusions covering the stubby central spadix

Marsh Marigold loves wet feet. Look for it in early spring along woodland creeks and in wooded swamps.

The Skunk Cabbage actually generates enough heat to melt the snow around it.

Emerging leaves will become gigantic fronds by midsummer, long after the flower has disappeared.

| March | April | May |

Central Heating

Snow often covers the forest floor when Skunk Cabbage first pushes up through the frozen ground. But in conditions that would kill other plants, this little trooper stokes the fires of its own "body" with stored energy from underground roots. Internal temps will remain at an amazing 68 degrees F, even on below-freezing nights. To maintain this "furnace," Skunk Cabbage must burn oxygen at an incredibly high rate. Research has shown that at near freezing temps, the plant is using O_2 at the same rate as a hovering hummingbird! The heat may also help waft its pungent odor to attract the flies and bees that pollinate it.

Huge summer-leaves help recharge Skunk Cabbage's underground "batteries."

BOREAL FOREST
The Canadian Carpet

Our Great Lakes boreal forest —also known as taiga or the sub-boreal forest—is a mosaic of cover including pockets of Quaking Aspen, beaver meadows, pine islands, Black Spruce bogs and ash and cedar swamps. Millions of acres of the forest is in the climax White Spruce-Balsam Fir stage. A climax forest can regenerate itself indefinitely until the next natural disaster changes the landscape.

Friendly Fire

Fire and wind—as we learned on July 4, 1999 when one of the largest blow-downs in history hit the canoe country —dramatically alter the composition of the northern forests. Late U.S. Forest Service ecologist Bud Heinselman's years of research on the fire history of the BWCAW (Boundary Waters Canoe Area Wilderness) can be boiled down to one simple fact: every part of the canoe country burned in a wildfire roughly every 100 years. Many species have adapted to this harsh reality. Jack Pine cones are serotinous, meaning they only open during forest fires. Heat of at least 116 degrees F melts the resin that holds the scales shut, thereby releasing the seeds into the fertile seed bed. The seeds of Pin Cherry, Bicknell's Geranium and Pale Corydalis can survive for decades in the soil, waiting for the next fire to open the canopy, warm the soil and release nutrients like phosphorous, calcium and magnesium. Bottom line— the boreal forest needs fire.

Charred lands of Minnesota's 1971 Little Indian Sioux fire supported 20,000 newly sprouted Jack Pine seedlings per acre! After a disturbance, pioneer trees such as Quaking Aspen, Paper Birch and Jack Pine, and pioneer herbaceous plants like Fringed Bindweed, Fireweed and Large-leafed Aster thrive. But eventually, if given enough disturbance-free time, the forest will return to a stable climax spruce-fir state. Red and White Pines depend on wildfires to keep competitors at bay. Thick bark protects the old pines from all but the most intense crown fires.

Meet the Canadian Carpet

The "Canadian carpet" is only a small number of species, but they comprise the vast majority of ground cover in the boreal forest.

Large-leaved Aster	20
Clintonia	21
Canada Mayflower	22
Twinflower	22
Bunchberry	23
Starflower	25
Pink Ladyslipper	26
Calypso	27
Spotted Coralroot	27
Pipsissewa	28
Wintergreen	30
One-flowered Wintergreen	30
Indian Pipe	30
Shinleaf	31
Pink Pyrola	31

Large-leaved Aster
Aster macrophyllus

Huge, hand-sized leaves nearly obscure the ground in areas of the North Woods. These are the first-year leaves of Large-leaved Aster. Very few of these plants will shoot up and flower in midsummer.

My favorite name for this plant is "lumberjack toilet paper;" though not big enough for Paul Bunyan's butt, the leaves do have a fair amount of surface area, are not irritating to sensitive skin and are quite abundant. Others know this plant by the more serious and less charming name—bigleaf aster.

Charming Deer

Ojibwa hunters in the Lake Superior region would smoke the plant before pursuing deer. They believed the smoke would attract the "four-leggeds."

Nature's Charmin®—large lower leaves can save you in a pinch. We recommend softer under side.

12 to 48 inches

Bee Bee-havior

Every autumn bees suffer from their own private energy crisis. All the "high-reward" flowers are done blooming. These were the gaudy, large-flowered blossoms that rewarded the foraging bees with much nectar: Fireweed, Jewelweed and Common Milkweed are examples. A bee's only September source for energy are low-reward flowers such as goldenrods and asters.

But the bees make a valiant attempt at late-season survival by feeding on Large-leaved Asters and relatives. If the day is cool, they may not be able to generate enough energy from the nectar to fly at all. Bumblebees make good on their name as they clumsily walk around on the plant; eventually falling to the ground, the last of their resources spent. Only the queen survives the winter.

July	August	Sept

Clintonia
Clintonia borealis

Clintonia, with its commanding presence and lily heritage, seems to be a domestic garden flower "gone native." But it's a 100 percent North Woods original. One of the few plants that is as striking in bloom as it is in berry. Clintonia grows in a wide variety of habitats in the North; it is common under nearly pure stands of Red Maple yet equally at home in lush carpets of Schreber's Moss (*Pleurozium schreberi*) under the dark cover of a Black Spruce-Northern White Cedar Swamp forest.

I've always called this plant Clintonia. Others call it blue-bead lily in reference to its beautiful but unpalatable blue berries. Early folk names such as bear-tongue, bear plum, Clinton's lily, wild-corn, hound's-tongue and dragoness plant have all but disappeared.

Thoreau wonderfully describes the Clintonia fruit he found on July 30, 1860, "The berries, which are of a peculiar dark, indigo blue (also like some kinds of blue china—some say "Amethystine blue") grow in umbels of two or five on the summits, very brittle stems eight to ten inches high, which break with a snap, and on erectish stemlets or pedicels. They are of singular form, oblong or squarish round, the size of large peas with a dimple atop."

Erie Coincidence?

This ubiquitous lily of the northern forests was named for an early governor of New York, DeWitt Clinton (born 1769…no relation to Bill), whose claim to fame was pushing through the construction of the Erie Canal. The proposed canal, from Lake Erie to the Hudson River, was laughingly known as "Clinton's Ditch" to his opponents.

A 1933 biography by Dorothie Bobbe stated that Clinton "excelled in zoology, botany, geology and mineralogy…. In ichthyology and ornithology his knowledge was minute." We also know that he was an honorary member of the prestigious Linnaean Society of London and a personal friend of most of the prominent naturalists and scientists of his day. At the time, he had one of the finest mineral collections in the country.

Clintonia

The young still-curled leaves make a decent salad green.

3 to 5 inches

Canada Mayflower

Ca
Mayfl
may b
most com
flower i
canoe cou

6 to 14 inches

| May | June | July |

| May | June | July |

During his political career with the Peace Party, Clinton fought for education, better conditions for the poor and the abolition of slavery. He sounds like a worthy namesake for this lovely yellow lily.

Salad for the Masses

The young, still curled leaves of spring make a decent salad, though, I must say, much better with a little ranch dressing. During settlement times, it was a very popular potherb for the "country people" of Maine who called it cow-tongue.

Not all Blue Berries are Blueberries

Clintonia's blue berries of midsummer can be easily mistaken for edible blueberries by children and unaware adults. It is important, though, that we know the difference since Clintonia berries are mildly poisonous.

Twinflower

2 to 4 inches

May	June	July

Canada Mayflower
Maianthemum canadense

I used to call this plant False Lily-of-the-Valley but have switched over to Canada Mayflower. It has a nicer ring to it, even though it sometimes doesn't bloom until June. Other folkloric names include elf-feather, dwarf Solomon's-seal, one-blade, heart leaf, scurvy berry and Solomon's-plume. The genus name is *Maianthemum* and literally translates to "May flower." Famed Quetico naturalist, the late Shan Walshe, crowned it, "the most common forest flower in Quetico." He found it on innumerable sites, from wet to very dry.

Mayflower berries stay green for a long while before turning a vivid red in autumn.

The pale-green speckled berries mature to a startling ruby-red in late fall. Mice, chipmunks and grouse eat them. Rabbits and hares eat the leaves. But humans should stay away as there is evidence that the berries are a strong purgative and may contain glycosides—a heart stimulant.

Twinflower
Linnaea borealis

Twinflower is a beautiful and delicate flower of the northern hemisphere's boreal and sub-boreal forests. It is one of the many flowers we share with Scandinavia. Two nodding, tiny pink flowers hang from every stalk, like Lilliputian lamp posts. A threadlike runner with paired, rounded leaves connects the flower stalks. The runner is nestled in the mossy beds where Twinflower is usually found. The flowers, though small and hard to get your nose up to, are wonderfully fragrant.

Linnaeus in Lapland

Famed Swedish botanist, Linnaeus first discovered Twinflower on a Swedish Academy of Sciences-sponsored expedition to Lapland in 1732. Though his description is less than glowing, "a little northern plant, long overlooked, depressed, abject, flowering early," Linnaeus loved the little Lapland beauty. Since no honorable botanist would ever name a plant after himself, Gronovius, his benefactor, graciously named it for him—*Linnaea borealis*. Linnaeus holds a sprig of Twinflower in his official portrait. The plant is still called *Linnea* in Norway and Sweden.

Botanical Beatitudes

Linnaeus truly was the father of binomial nomenclature and modern plant systematics. His *Genera Plantarum* of 1753 was the first work to organize the plant kingdom by sexual characteristics. Basically unchanged in 250 years, it is still in use today. But he was also a popular naturalist. His flora hikes through the Swedish countryside attracted great crowds—so many people, in fact, that he'd have a band of trumpets and French horns play when he wanted to step up on his box and share a botanical beatitude.

The great Carl Linnaeus, holding his namesake, Linnaea borealis.

Bunchberry
Cornus canadensis

This plant can fool you. It appears to be a small herbaceous plant with one large, white four-petaled flower that produces tasty red berries. Wait, "berries" plural? How can one flower produce a dozen or more berries? It can't. The Bunchberry "flower" is actually four white bracts surrounding a cluster of 20 to 30 miniscule greenish flowers. The showy white bracts probably attract the attention of pollinating insects, like bees, which would otherwise ignore the tiny green flowers. And what about those tasty berries? The truth is that the berry is technically a drupe; a mealy fruit with large stones inside. Note also that

Bunchberry

Flower-bearing plants have six leaves; those without flowers have only four.

Grouse, chipmunks and Rock Voles relish bunchberry fruit. American Robins, Veerys, Philadelphia and Warbling Vireos also feed on the bright red drupes.

3 to 6 inches

| May | June | July |

blooming plants have six leaves while plants without blossoms only have four. What gives? It could be that the two extra leaves are required for photosynthesis to support the higher energy demands of flowering.

Quetico naturalist Shan Walshe noted that Bunchberry is one of the few plants able to survive in the highly acidic Sphagnum Moss carpets in old growth Black Spruce forests.

Others have known this ground-hugging plant as frothberry, crackerberry, cuckoo-plum, low cornel, pudding berry and trailing dogwood. Dogwood bushes are actually the larger cousins of this small woody plant of the same family.

Pollination Explosion

As an alternative to insects, Bunchberry seems to rely on self-fertilization. Flower buds open suddenly causing the anthers to spring up and shed pollen into the air. This may be enough to fertilize some of its near neighbors. The trigger for this "explosion" is a tiny 5/32"-long structure near the tip of one of the four flower petals.

A Pleasant Nibble

The pulpy, white-fleshed berry-like drupes with a slightly sweet taste are appreciated by some human nibblers (beware the stony seeds). If you don't find snacking on Bunchberry berries pleasing, why not try boiling them into a pudding and eating them with cream and sugar?

Shade Garden Superstar

Bunchberry was introduced into England in 1774 as an exotic new garden flower. The lowly plant from the North Woods became the star of English shade gardens. The Brits eventually bestowed on this humble little northern plant the Royal Horticultural Society Award of Merit in 1937.

Starflower

Bunchberries are often found in large groups that absolutely carpet the ground. These stands can actually be a single colony, all connected and spreading by underground horizontal roots called rhizomes.

Starflower
Trientalis borealis

Neither gaudy nor garish, Starflower is a modest member of the Canadian Carpet crew. The Swedes affectionately call it *skogstjarna*, or "wood star." I loved the name so much that I christened my land *Skogstjarna* (not to be confused with John Denver's "Star wood in Aspen"). Old names for the plant include star-of-Bethlehem, star anemone, Maystar and chick wintergreen.

The last name was evidently despised by author Susan Cooper, who wrote in 1850, "[It] is an insult to the plant, and to the common sense of the community. Why, it is one of the daintiest wood-flowers, with nothing in the world to do with chicks, or weeds, or winter. It is not the least of an evergreen, its leaves withering in autumn…and there is not a chicken in the country that knows it by sight or taste."

Heptandric.

4 to 8 inches

Skogstjarna is the lovely Swedish name for this plant. It means "wood star."

Fleshy underground tubers store energy to give Starflower an early season energy boost.

Starflower usually bears flowers with seven petals and stems with seven leaves. Occasionally they will have six or eight petals or leaves

May	June	July

Starflower is one of the few plants that regularly shows seven petals, seven stamens, seven sepals and seven leaves—a very odd pattern in a kingdom where flower parts in 3s, 4s and 6s are the norm. The great botanist, Carl Linnaeus, in his original classification of plants by sexual system, placed Starflower in class Heptandra, a very small group of seven-parted species. But look closely…many Starflowers have six or eight leaves and six or eight petals.

Pink Ladyslipper
Cypripedium acaule

Contrary to the beliefs of many, this is not the Minnesota state flower. I personally feel it should be as it is just as pretty as the Showy Ladyslipper (*Cypripedium reginae*), grows in wilder locations and is more widespread than the Showy.

Moccasin flower is a very popular common name and may have come from the Native American word for the orchid. Other names include Indian-moccasin, camel's-foot, stemless lady-slipper, purple-slipper, Whip-poor-will's-shoes, Noah's-ark and old-goose.

Buzzing Blossoms

The sound stopped me in my tracks…the ladyslipper was buzzing! Turns out, a large bumble-bee had entered the "slipper" and gotten quite stuck. Orchids are very particular about their polli-nators, and this big fat bee was not on this Pink Ladyslipper's guest list. In a study of 456 orchid species, over 80 percent accommodated only one or two pollinating species!

Bees enter the Ladyslipper pouch by the "front door" but must exit by the "back door" where pollination takes place.

The "front door"

All orchids have leaves with parallel veins.

6 to 15 inches

Our Pink Ladyslipper is cleverly designed for two small bees: leaf-cutting bees (*Megachile* species) and mining bees (*Andrena* species). They are attracted by a mock nectar scent and squeeze into the slipper-like pouch to find the source. Once inside, the tiny bees eat the droplets off some hairs and then try to exit by the same door they entered, but the slippery walls and overhanging lip prevent escape. Instead they must exit by the rear door where they are slapped on the back by the pollen-sack from the anthers. At the next ladyslipper the pollen sack is scraped off the bee's back by the bristly stigma. "Mission Pollination" accomplished!

May	June	July

The Pink Ladyslipper prefers cool, shadowy Sphagnum and Feather Moss beds.

Calypso
Calypso bulbosa

This rare jewel of an orchid is protected by its remote cedar swamp habitat and fickle blooming nature. *Calypso* translates to "hidden"—an appropriate name for a plant that is often concealed in the darkest cedar forests. Some call it fairyslipper orchid.

Calypso is named for the goddess daughter of Atlas: Homer's beautiful nymph. She was hidden on the island of Ogygia and discovered by Ulysses when he became shipwrecked.

Muir's Memories
John Muir's second greatest day was when he met Ralph Waldo Emerson in Yosemite National Park. The American environmentalist's greatest moment? The day he discovered Calypso blooming in a Canadian cedar-bog.

3 to 6 inches

May	June	July

Spotted Coralroot
Corallorhiza maculata

Look for clumps of these red-stemmed little orchids on the shaded floor of a mixed coniferous-deciduous forest. Surprisingly, the red stems do not immediately jump out at you from the shadowed ground. But diligence pays off, and a little effort will reward you with a close look at some very cool flowers.

You Big Sap
These striking, but often overlooked, orchids are true saprophytes. They get all their nutrients from decaying organic matter in the soil. Since they do not need the sun to photosynthesize and make food, they have no green leaves; in fact, they barely have leaves at all.

The "coralroots" are a mass of thick rhizomes entwined with the mycorhizal threads of a fungus that act as the delivery boy, bringing nutrients directly to the plant. The fungus, in turn, is living off decaying matter in the soil.

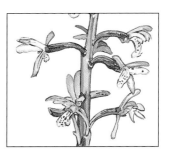

Green Leaves? We don't need no stinkin' green leaves! Coralroot gets all its nutrients "hand delivered" by fungi in the soil.

6 to 12 inches

May	June	July

Pipsissewa
Chimaphila umbellata

One of the few plants that retains its original, or nearly original, native name; in this case a beautiful Cree word that rolls off the tongue —*Pipsissewa*. The Ojibwa call it *gagigebug* or "everlasting leaf."

Home Remedies
Ojibwa healers treated sore eyes with drops made from a root decoction.

4 to 8 inches

Native knowledge was passed on to the colonists and resulted, eventually, in accepted home remedies. Pipsissewa tonic was used to treat skin irritations and bruises and was even listed on the *U.S. Pharmacopoeia* from 1820 to 1916.

Botanist Frederick Pursh writes in 1814, "The plant is in high esteem for its medicinal qualities among the natives; they call it *sip-si-sewa*. I have myself been witness of a successful cure made by a decoction of this plant, in a very severe case of hysteria. It is a plant eminently deserving the attention of physicians."

Stone Breaker
Formerly, it was believed that Pipsissewa had properties that could break down kidney stones. In fact, the Cree name for this plant means, "it breaks into small pieces." But modern science finds this doubtful, although it does conclude that it is a mild urinary antiseptic.

June	July	August

Wintergreen
Gaultheria procumbens

Wintergreen is a small unobtrusive plant of dark coniferous forest moss beds. Look for thick waxy leaves that are a deep dark green. Henry David Thoreau commented that Wintergreen appears to "never bloom, [the flowers] looking almost like snow-white berries." The

The urn-shaped flowers hang shyly under the canopy of the waxy leaves.

true berry forms in late summer but really comes into its own in autumn when it turns deep red.

The francophones of Quebec call this plant *petit thé dubois*, meaning "small tea of the woods." Checkerberry, teaberry, chickberry, foxberry, ivory plums, oneberry, partridge berry, spice-berry, young come-ups and winterberry are some early folk names for this very popular plant.

July	August	Sept

Better than Certs®

Spruce Grouse and chipmunks nibble on the berries, and so can you. They make a refreshing snack. If you see red berries on the plant in spring and early summer, you know they are last year's fruits that have survived the winter; try them now as winter frosts have nicely mellowed their flavor.

The Boston Tea Party

Wintergreen tea is a delightful drink that probably helped save the sanity of the colonists after the Boston Tea Party and the ensuing boycott on English tea. It was gathered in huge quantities and sold in Boston markets. Fortunately for this little heath, it was quite common in southeast Massachusetts at the time and survived the onslaught.

Oil of Wintergreen

The strong taste and sweet scent of a crushed leaf comes from the essential oil of wintergreen: 99 percent methyl salicylate and the terpene, gaultherilene. It was used to flavor candies, gum, cough drops and to hide the bitter taste of yesteryear's medicines. It took one ton of Wintergreen leaves to make a pound of oil! Fortunately, a synthetic substitute arrived on the scene in the nick of time.

Yellow Birch (*Betula lenta*) contains the exact same fragrant oil as Wintergreen. In the spring and summer, scratch the bark of a young Yellow Birch twig with your fingernail and inhale the wonderful fragrance.

2 to 5 inches

Wintergreen berries form in late summer; many survive the winter and can be found well into spring.

| May | June | July |

One-flowered Wintergreen
Moneses uniflora

Cool, dark, mossy forests are where this tiny pyrola prefers to chill. Canadians often refer to this lilliput of the forest as "single delight." In fact, the genus *Moneses* is derived from two Greek words *monos* meaning "one" and *hesia* which means "delight." "Olav's candlestick" is the name Norwegians give to the plant while their neighbors, the Swedes, call it *ogonljus* or "eyelight."

2 to 4 inches

Delightful Relief

The Haida of the Pacific Northwest believed Pipsissewa to be powerful medicine and prescribed it for serious illnesses such as severe diarrhea, small pox and, what we today call cancer.

Indian Pipe
Monotropa uniflora

Who doesn't love this plant? Indian Pipe seems to me to be a rebel amongst flowers. It calmly seems to say, "Hey, you guys can all be green; I don't care…. I'm waxy white and proud of it." It is always a treat to find a cluster of the luminous stems glowing from the dark and shadowy forest floor.

Indian Pipe depends on a mushroom for its nutrition.

Corpses, Convulsions and Ghosts

Ghost flower, corpse plant, convulsion weed, fairy smoke, Dutchman's pipe, one-flowered waxplant and ice plant are other vernacular names for the bizarre flower.

Dr. Millspaugh believed "corpse plant" to be a fine name for a flower, "so like is it to the general bluish waxy appearance of the dead; then, too, it is cool and clammy to the touch, and rapidly decomposes and turns black even when carefully handled."

4 to 10 inches

Freeloading Fungus

Wandering down the portage path, this ghostly white plant is easily noticed. But how can this be a flowering plant? It's not green at all. Completely lacking in chlorophyll, it can't manufacture food from the sun. So how does it survive? The answer lies underground. It gets its nutrition from neighboring trees! The roots of an intermediary fungus (a *Boletus* species of mushroom) taps into living spruce roots and delivers nutrients to the coiled roots of the Indian Pipe.

June	July	August

Unlike the green Sphagnum Moss growing at its base, Indian Pipe is completely lacking in chlorophyll.

In fact, the roots are so entwined with the mycorrhizae (fungal roots) that they barely contact the soil. White stringy roots of Bolete mushrooms (the delivery boy) directly hand off food from the spruce (grocery store) to the Indian Pipe (the customer).

Due to this "lazy" method of securing nourishment, some early botanists disdained this innocent flower for its "degenerate morals."

Clear Eyes, Clear Mind
Ojibwa healers believed the clear sap from the stem could clear up cloudy vision. The Cherokee made a soothing eye wash from the sap mixed with water.

Fungal Forecaster
If the Thompson Indians of British Columbia noticed a proliferation of Indian Pipe in the woods, they looked forward to an abundance of mushrooms come late summer and fall.

Shinleaf *Pyrola elliptica*

Look for the stalk of waxy, cup-shaped nodding flowers under a canopy of mixed coniferous and deciduous trees. The Latin, *Pyrola*, is in reference to the resemblance of this plant's leaves to pear tree leaves (*Pyrus* species).

It is commonly called shinleaf but has been called liverleaf, wintergreen and rheumatism-weed. Both pyrola species are found in the dappled-light understory of mixed forests.

Rheumatism-weed
Since pyrola leaves have analgesic properties, they were commonly used to treat sores, cuts and bruises. Native Americans knew it as an effective treatment for rheumatism.

Waxy evergreen leaves sprout from the base of all pyrolas.

May	June	July

Pink Pyrola *Pyrola asarifolia*

5 to 10 inches

6 to 15 inches

Pink Pyrola

May	June	July

Shinleaf

NORTHERN BOGS
Sphagnum Moss Mats & Black Spruce Bogs

Bogs are not only deep, dark mosquito-infested swamps where, if you're not careful, you'll be sucked down and your body preserved in the muck for centuries, but also places of light where Palm Warblers nest, delicate pink orchids grow and some of the most fascinating plants on earth make their home.

Ice Age Origins
Bogs are relics of the Ice Age. Melted glacial ice filled depressions in the bedrock 11,000 years ago. Gradually, mats of intertwined roots and deep blankets of Sphagnum Mosses grow out and over the stagnant pools. There is no outlet or inlet. Swamps fill from the bottom up; bogs grow in from the sides and fill down. On these floating margins one can gently bounce up and down as if on a giant waterbed…, and I guess that's basically what it is. Peat soil underlays all bogs. It is a conglomerate of poorly decomposed organic matter.

But the forest is encroaching. In concentric rings around the open water you'll find a floating Sphagnum mat with Pitcher Plants, sundews and orchids, a shrub zone of Leatherleaf, Bog Birch and stunted Black Spruce, and the outer ring, which is a climax spruce-fir forest that will eventually reclaim the bog.

Cold Deserts
Bogs are cold deserts. Desiccation (drying out) is a serious problem for plants in this ecosystem. Winter winds steal precious moisture in an environment that is already very "un-humid." Roots locked in ice for up to eight months a year are unable to take up water. Some plants use thick evergreen leaves and waxy coatings to reduce water loss. The stomates ("breathing" cells) of certain bog plants remain "closed for the season" to help retain H_2O.

N and P Demands
Nutrients are hard to come by in a substrate of sterile moss. Nitrogen and phosphorous are the elements especially in demand by plants. Bogs are highly acidic places due to the tannic acid from spruce, fir and pine needles that concentrate in these closed systems. Acidity retards the growth of bacteria and fungi. A short growing seasons and cool temps limits mites and springtails —key agents of breakdown. Decomposition, which releases nitrogen into the soil, is dependent on all these factors. The result? A nitrogen-poor environment where some plants resort to carnivory to get their essential nutrients.

Pitcher Plant
Sarracenia purpurea

Every floating bog worth its moss harbors a few Pitcher Plants. They are the quintessential bog plant, and I never get tired of searching for them. The strange-looking flower has a flattened pistil-head shielding the stamens. The "pitchers" are actually modified leaves and never cease to fascinate folks. Northern peoples have called this bog oddity by many names: bog-bugle, Adam's-pitcher, Adam's-cup, devil's-boot, fever-cup, fly-trap, frog-bonnet, Indian-jug, Indian-pipe, small pox plant, St. Jacob's-dipper, water-cup and Whip-poor-will's shoes. All are great names.

John Josselyn in 1672 wondered at the "hollow-leaved lavendar" with "one straight stalk about the bigness of an oat straw, better than a cubit

8 to 18 inches

The Pitcher Plant flower has a bizarre flattened pistil head which shields the stamens.

high; upon the top standeth one fantastical flower, the leaves grow close from the root, in shape like a tankard, hollow, tough, and always full of water."

You can age Pitcher Plant leaves by counting backwards. Gently part the moss to access the main stalk. The youngest leaves are attached at the highest point on the stem; older leaves below.

| May | June | July |

My Kind of Honor

Michel Sarrazin, a doctor in Quebec in the early 1700s, used this plant to treat small pox. To honor him, Linnaeus named the genus *Sarracenia* after him. The surgeon-general of New France's army was also the first person to perform a mastectomy in Canada, and possibly the world. He performed the feat in 1700.

Club Dead

Pitcher Plants produce extrafloral nectar to attract insects. The highest concentration is on the lower lip of first-year pitchers, but some is also produced on the veins of the hood. Glands on the epidermis produce this sweet attractant. Older pitchers do not produce much nectar compared to younger ones.

Insects, lured to the pitcher's lip begin feeding. If they walk down into the leaf to check it out, they find that their tiny little insect-feet are being coated in globs of loose platelets. Movement becomes difficult. "Time to get out of this creepy place," they think. But upon turning around, they notice, much to their chagrin, that all the pitcher hairs are pointing down. One slip and its all over; into the deadly cocktail they go.

The slippery inward-curving walls have them trapped. After they drown and sink to the bottom, their body is dissolved by a mixture of rain, fungi, bacteria, protozoans and a weak enzyme solution produced by the plant. Nitrogen, that is nearly absent in the bog environment, is absorbed from the insect carcass by special cells in the base of the pitcher.

One Man's Death Pool is another Man's Paradise

Not all captured critters become plant snacks. Amazingly, seventeen species of arthropods are able to survive and thrive

Insects are lured to the pitcher's lip by scented nectar.

Globs of slippery, loose platelets coat the feet of insects that investigate.

Downward-facing hairs prevent the critters from escaping.

Slick, inward facing walls precipitate a fall...

...into the death pool where they drown and are dissolved into a digestible slurry.

in the death pool. Critters found in the pitchers include bacteria, rotifers, cladocerans and larval stages of several flies including a species of Sarcophagus Fly (*Blaesoxipha fletcheri* of the Sarcophagidae), Pitcher Plant Midges (*Metriocnemus knabi* of the Chironomidae) and most notoriously, the Bog Mosquitoes (*Wyeomyia smithii* of the Culicidae). All have special adaptations that allow them to survive in this hostile environment.

The female Bog Mosquito uses special hooks on its feet to back down the slick pitcher wall, allowing her to lay enzyme-resistant eggs in the death pool. Developing larvae feed on protozoans in

A Vegetable Ant-Eater

A study of Pitcher Plant capture rates in Newfoundland, Canada by researchers from Stephen Heard University of Iowa found that, by weight, nearly 70 percent of the invertebrates caught were ants and slugs. Of the 4780 individual victims, 33 percent were ants, 33 percent flies, 8 percent slugs and 7 percent beetles. The average pitcher caught 11mg of prey over its lifetime.

A study by James Cresswell of the University of Michigan expanded on this and ranked all captured invertebrate groups by percentage of the total biomass of prey caught:

- Grasshoppers 37 percent
- Flies 15 percent
- Dragonflies 15 percent
- Beetles 14 percent
- Ants, bees and true bugs 9 percent

Though only 9 percent of biomass, ants, bees and true bugs (Hymenoptera and Homoptera) accounted for 28 percent of the individuals caught. This coincides nicely with the Newfoundland research that tallied 33 percent of Pitcher Plant victims as Hymenoptera.

the pitcher. A Florida State University study found an average of 20.7 Bog Mosquito larvae per inhabited pitcher.

Pupating at the bottom of the pitcher is the maggot of the Sarcophogus Fly. It avoids dissolution by secreting an anti-enzyme.

The black-and-yellow pitcher plant moths (*Exyra* species) lay a single egg in a pitcher. After hatching, developing caterpillars get down to the business of eating and, in the process, re-roof and drain their funky new home. First a dense layer of silk is produced, and then, as they chow on the inner walls, part of the pitcher collapses creating a roofed and cozy shelter. Now they cut two doors—one for drainage and one for exiting as an adult moth.

Spider Substrate

Spiders are considered "resource parasites" of Pitcher Plants because their webs block pitcher mouths and thereby prevent the plant from capturing insects and other invertebrates. James Cresswell of the University of Michigan found spider webs in 30 percent of the pitchers studied.

Round-leaved Sundew
Drosera rotundifolia

Most folks are surprised how tiny sundew is when they first encounter it nestled amongst the fronds of moss in a northern bog. Contrary to most plants, the leaves of sundew are more widely recognized than the flowers. The leaves bristle with glistening dew-covered stalks while the miniscule flowers only bloom one at a time and for a very short while.

"Sundew" is believed to come from corruption of the Saxon word *sin dew*, meaning "constantly dewy," an apropos name, indeed. Various colloquial names have been attributed to sundew: bed-rot, dew-grass, dew plant, eyebright, moonwort, moor-grass, youth-root and youthwort.

"It's not Dew...It's Glue"

Charles "Evolution" Darwin was fascinated by this aggressive little carnivore with the innocuous name; he eventually published a book about them and their hungry plant cousins called *Insectivorous*

Extremely sensitive, sticky-tipped hairs respond to the slightest weight and can distinguish edible prey from rain, twigs or dirt.

Plants in 1897. He discovered that the sticky-tipped hairs responded to items as small as a piece of hair 2/10 of a millimeter long and weighing a miniscule 0.000822 milligrams. This is even more sensitive than the human tongue. And sundews can somehow discriminate between edible material and inedible items such as tiny twig fragments, dirt and raindrops. As the victim struggles, held fast by the "glue," the leaf closes around it creating a temporary stomach for digestion. Darwin was the first scientist to prove that plants can digest animal matter. Inside the folded leaves, acid, similar to the gastric juices found in animal stomachs, is secreted. Protein from the victim's body is broken down into nitrogen-rich compounds that are essential to plant growth.

Pollination of sundew flowers is performed by the same insects — mosquitoes, gnats and midges—that the plants eat!

3 to 6 inches

Most of us know the leaves of sundew better than its flower.

Cough Suppressant

Round-leaved Sundew contains spasmolytic and antimicrobial properties that are used by herbalists to treat asthma and whooping cough in children. This knowledge is not new; William Turner reported in 1568 that Englishmen "holde that it is good for consumptions and swooning and faintness of the harte." In 1887 many medical writers recommend its use for "different kinds of coughs, arising from bronchial attacks…and other diseases of the lungs." Today, sundew pills for the relief of coughs that are "worse when lying down" are sold at natural food stores.

| May | June | July |

IMPOSTER ALERT!
Bog Scheuchzeria

Scheuchzeria palustris *is not truly a wildflower, a sedge or a rush. So what the heck is it? This bog oddity is actually a podgrass...not a grass...a podgrass. It is the only North American member of the podgrass family— the Scheuchzerieaceae (say that with a mouth full of popcorn!). Blame the name on the person that dedicated this plant to Swiss botanist John Jakob Scheuchzer.*

Look for the 10-inch zigzag stem and the clusters of pod-like capsules (actually follicles) in groups of three.

Floating bogs from Alaska to New Jersey are home to Bog Scheuchzeria. It is called Rannoch Rush in Scotland.

| June | July | August |

Buckbean or Bogbean
Menyanthes trifoliata

Shallow waters of acidic bogs is the favored haunt of this unique plant. Buckbean is commonly called bogbean (especially in England and Ireland) and has formerly been known by these aliases: marsh clover, water shamrock, bean trefoil, brook bean, bog myrtle, *bocks boonen* (Flemish for "the goat's bean") and *vattenklover* ("water clover" in Swedish). It not only graces the bogs of the Canadian Shield but also grows in the moors of England, Scotland and mainland Europe.

Menyanthes is a name given this plant by Linnaeus. It literally means "month flower" implying it blooms for a month. June is the month in the North Woods. The last part of its Latin name, *trifoliata*, refers to the three-parted leaves.

Wet feet are no problem for the Buckbean. It prefers the soggier bogs.

Pretty in Pink
Pink-tinged blossoms soften the image of this bog plant with the horrible name. In 1633, Gerarde, an author and naturalist, poetically wrote of its inflorescence, "a bush of feather-like floures of a white colour, dasht ouer slightly with a wash of light carnation." Curly hairs make the flowers look delicately fringed.

The late summer green fruits of Buckbean.

May	June	July

6 to 12 inches

Arthritis Healer?
Holistic-online.com lists *Menyanthes trifoliata* as a "most useful herb for the treatment of rheumatism, osteo-arthritis and rheumatoid arthritis." It goes on to say that it is an excellent aid to promoting digestion by increasing the production of gastric juices and bile flow. Its active compounds include anthraquinone derivatives and flavonoid glycosides.

Historically this potent herb has been used as a tobacco, a dressing to dissolve "glandular swellings," a tea (mixed with wormwood or sage) to cure dyspepsia and an extract to treat and prevent rheumatism and scurvy. In fact, its German name *scharbock* is a corruption of the Latin *scorbutus*, which means "scurvy."

Missen Bread
The Sami (Laplanders) of northern Scandinavia made a bread from the rhizomes. It was called *missen*, or famine bread.

Small-fruited Bog Cranberry
Vaccinium oxycoccus

Small-fruited Bog Cranberry grows in cold bogs around the northern hemisphere from the North Woods east to Scandinavia and Siberia. Tiny erect plants spring up out of the Sphagnum Moss intermittently along a trailing woody stem up to four feet in length. The delicate pink flowers with the swept back petals are rarely seen but well worth the wet feet needed to access their haunts.

As a member of the Heath family, cranberry is a first cousin to the blueberry but totally unrelated to the familiar shrub, Highbush Cranberry (*Viburnum trilobum*).

The Ojibwa plucked cranberries from the autumn bog in great numbers, drying and storing them for winter use. In fact, so valuable were these properties, the Ojibwa clans would pass down their best wild cranberry bogs from generation to generation.

Frost—Cranberry's Best Buddy
Cranberries are best collected after the first hard frosts in fall. Why that late? Freezing releases sugars that cuts the berry's tartness and makes them palatable. The best time to tramp out into the bogs for wild cranberries is in October. Benzoic acid in the berry acts as a preservative and bactericide allowing some berries to survive the winter intact. I have eaten last year's berries in May and they were still delicious.

2 to 4 inches

"Cranberry" may be a corruption of "crane berry" as the flower and stalk somewhat resemble the beak, head and neck of a crane or heron.

| May | June | July |

The Corporate Cranberry
Your grocery-bought cranberry juice is made from the domestic relative of our Large-fruited Bog Cranberry (*V. macrocarpon*). These wild cranberries of the wild northern bogs were first domesticated in 1810. Today, they are a valuable agricultural crop. Wisconsin, Washington and Massachusetts are the nation's leaders in cranberry production.

A Royal Gift
The natives regaled the Pilgrims that first fall with a new tart and tasty berry—the cranberry. In fact, they were considered so valuable that the loyal settlers chose the tiny red berries over precious Beaver pelts and even more valuable White Pine timber as a gift to their king in England. I hope he liked tart!

Bog Birch

Bog Birch, **Betula glandulifera,** *is actually a shrub related to the tree—Paper Birch* (**Betula papyrifera**). *The harsh growing conditions in floating bogs limit its size to barely three or four feet. Its miniature waxy leaves and tiny catkins are soooo cute. The flame red leaves brighten the bog in autumn.*

Early Ojibwa healers burned the tiny cone-like female catkins creating an aromatic smoke to clear up swollen mucous membranes.

A tea made from the catkins was believed to give women strength during child bearing.

Arethusa
Arethusa bulbosa

Arethusa is also known as dragon's mouth, moss nymph and wild pink. *Arethusa bulbosa* loves sunny floating bogs.

Arethusa is the only species of its genus in North America. Another *Arethusa* species is found in Japan.

Some have unflatteringly described the flower head as resembling the open mouth of a braying ass. I object. A delicate beauty such as Arethusa should never have to suffer such indignation.

Deceptive Dragon.

If I could be a bumblebee, I would certainly make a beeline for the sweet-smelling and pretty-pink Arethusa. Unfortunately, there would be little reward in the form of nectar as this plant produces very little. Therefore, Arethusa must rely on fooling inexperienced bumblebees, tricking them into landing on itself and, in

the process, getting pollinated. Reliance on young bumblebees for pollination forces Arethusa's bloom phenology to match the emergence dates of young bumblebees.

Nymph of Fountains

The nymph Arethusa was minding her own business, bathing in the river, when Alpheus, the River god, saw her and desired her. He chased Arethusa but Artemis, the goddess of women, had pity and changed her into an underground stream. From that point on, Arethusa was known as the nymph of fountains.

4 to 8 inches

| May | June | July |

Rose Pogonia
Pogonia ophioglossoides

You're going to get your knees wet when you drop down to admire this delicate denizen of floating Sphagnum bog mats. The pink orchid with the bearded tongue (more on this later) is fairly common in June. If you can't wait until June, then head south to Georgia's Okefenokee Swamp where it blooms in April. Rose Pogonia is the only member of the genus in North America. Its range includes most of the eastern states from Ontario and Minnesota east to Nova Scotia and Newfoundland, south to central Florida and west to Texas. Soil conditions seem to be the limiting factor and not temperature. It needs an acidic environment. A rare white form is occasionally observed.

"Rose" is also known by the awful name, "bearded snake tongue orchid." But this is simply a literal translation of its Latin name *Pogonia ophioglossoides*. The genus name *Pogonia* means "bearded" in Greek and refers to its fuzzy lip. The Latin root of *ophioglossoides* is "snake" (*ophio*) and "tongue" or "mouth" (*gloss*).

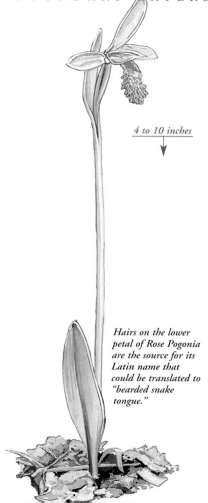

4 to 10 inches

Hairs on the lower petal of Rose Pogonia are the source for its Latin name that could be translated to "bearded snake tongue."

Rose Pogonias, the Poem
> "For though the grass was scattered
> Yet every second spear
> Seemed tipped with wings of color
> That tinged the atmosphere."
> —Robert Frost

What's that Snaky Smell?
Henry David Thoreau wrote in 1852, "the adder's-tongue arethusa smells exactly like a snake. How singular that in nature, too, beauty and offensiveness should be thus combined! In flowers, as well as in men, we demand a beauty pure and fragrant, which perfumes the air. The flower, which is showy but has no, or an offensive, odor expresses the character of too many mortals." Henry thought this little orchid smelled exactly like a snake. I don't know about you, but I don't go around smelling snakes. But, hey, to each his own. Actually, the foul smell has been attributed only to withered blossoms.

May	June	July

Grass-Pink or Swamp-Pink
Calopogon tuberosus

What a treat it is to find this brazenly pink orchid standing proud in its mucky surroundings. Grass-Pink and Rose Pogonia are often cozy neighbors on the floating Sphagnum mats of northern bogs. Not exclusively a North Woods species, Grass-Pink grows as far south as the acidic wetlands of Florida, though it is now only found in six or seven locations there. It is also known as Swamp-Pink.

Topsy-Turvy

Minnesota naturalist Raphael Carter wonderfully describes Grass-Pink as "a wild rose torn to bits, then glued back together by someone who had never seen a flower before."

Though this flower looks like it grew upside down, it is actually all other orchids that are topsy-turvy. Most orchid flowers first develop with the lip at the top and then twist 180

Upside down orchids. The lower lip of Grass-Pink stays at the top.

4 to 12 inches

degrees as it fully blooms; this is called resupinate development. Grass-Pink on the other hand is non-resupinate, foregoing "the twist," preferring to keep its lip on top, thank you.

Trick Landing

Yellow hairs on the lip are mock stamens that help attract bees. When the bee lands—often a carpenter bee (*Xylocopa* species) — the hinged lip collapses, putting the bee on its back and right on top of the column. Here it picks up the sticky pollina or transfers pollen from another Grass-Pink.

June	July	August

2 to 10 inches above water

Greater Bladderwort
Utricularia vulgaris

Pretty little yellow flower heads peek up above the surface of the bog pond, appearing innocent and benign, but underwater the roots harbor dozens of death chambers.

Henry David Thoreau, known to not mince his words, decried the deception and described bladderwort as a "dirty-conditioned flower, like a sluttish woman with a gaudy yellow bonnet."

May	June	July

Our six bladderwort species all overwinter as buds that have sunk to the bottom muck of the bog pond.

Falsely Imprisoned?

It is commonly believed that bladderwort plants get much of their nutrition from captured microscopic aquatic life (zooplankton). The below-water bladders have one-way trap doors that let zooplankton in but not out. Miniscule hairs help sort out who's who. The tiny little victims are dissolved within the bladders and their nutrients absorbed by the plant. One North Woods species, Purple Bladderwort (*Utricularia purpurea*), is more than 25 percent bladders by mass.

Surprisingly, research has shown that the bladders may catch and eat very few microinvertebrates. In these bladders live happy little communities of algae and zooplankton. Studies by Amanda Bern at Florida International University on Leafy Bladderwort (*Utricularia foliosa*) support this. It was found that only 0.44 percent of needed nitrogen and 1.75 percent of required phosphorus were from captured critters. They could even grow without any bladder traps at all! In fact, plants without bladders showed higher nitrogen rates than those with bladders.

The bladders are the small, reddish blobs connected to the underwater stems.

Doorway

Trigger hairs

This is a greatly magnified view of a single bladder. A one-way trap door lets zooplankton in but not out. Miniscule hairs serve as triggers and can distinguish prey from aquatic detritus.

Black Spruce Bogs

The six species that follow all hang out in Black Spruce bogs. What is the difference between this type of bog and a floating sphagnum bog? Time. The Black Spruce Bog is simply a floating bog that has completely grown over and filled down to form enough of a substrate for the trees to grow on.

Early stages of this type of bog are covered with small Black Spruce and Tamarack. Due to the nutrient poor soils and very acidic environment, many are stunted. A Black Spruce of two-inches in diameter may be 100 years old! Further out on the edges of the bog, the trees are able to grow larger on the better soils.

Black Spruce can be separated from White Spruce by its bog habitat (it likes its feet wet), shorter needles ($1/2$ inch) and scraggly profile. White Spruce grows tall and full on upland sites and has one-inch needles.

Juncos, Palm Warblers, Lincoln's Sparrows and Yellow-bellied Flycatchers make this habitat their residence of choice.

Bog Solomon's-Seal
Smilacina trifolia

Don't confuse this sphagnum-dwelling plant of the deep and dark bogs with its larger cousin of the deciduous woods—Solomon's Seal. It is most common in Black Spruce bogs that contain Northern White Cedar or Tamarack.

It is also commonly known as Three-leaved Solomon's-Seal.

Thrushes, grouse and mice are known to eat the berries of this northern plant.

| May | June | July |

3 to 8 inches

Dark mossy beds in Black Spruce forests is where Bog Solomon's Seal is most at home.

Bog Rosemary
Andromeda glaucophylla

Bog Rosemary is a circumpolar species found in spruce bogs around the globe from northern Saskatchewan to Scandinavia to Siberia. The pinkish nodding flowers open only slightly making them appear to be perpetually in the flower bud stage. They are pollinated by honeybees, bumblebees and mining bees (*Andrena* species). The leaves may bear a slight resemblance to the well known, but totally unrelated, culinary herb—rosemary. Several plants may sprout from a single rhizome.

My Big Fat Greek Name
This genus is named for Andromeda the Greek goddess daughter of Cepheus and Cassiope of Ethiopia. When her mother boasted that she was more beautiful than the Nereid nymphs of the Mediterranean, Poseidon grew angry and sent a sea monster to destroy the land. Andromeda was chained to a rock as a sacrifice but Perseus rescued her before the sea monster had a beautiful lunch. She married her rescuer.

The specific epithet is *glaucophylla*, which is Latin for "bright bluish-green leaved."

Weed or Wonderful?
I found a web page called "Wisconsin Cranberry Weeds" sponsored by the Wisconsin State Cranberry Growers Association. Under the Bog Rosemary heading it laments that it "easily invades older, established cranberry beds. If not restricted, Bog Rosemary can form large dense patches and compete with cranberry vines for sunlight and nutrients." Perspective is everything when it comes to labeling a flowering plant a "weed."

| May | June | July |

Bog Laurel
Kalmia polifolia

Bog Laurel is a pink -flowered heath of Black Spruce bogs with a pH of between 4.5 and 5.0. It grows alongside Bog Rosemary in sun-dappled moss beds. Some folks call it swamp laurel. The native Swede, Pehr "Peter" Kalm, was one of the pioneers of Canadian botany. In his honor the genus of this plant—*Kalmia*—was named after him. He wrote in November 1748, "Dr. Linné [Linnaeus], because of the peculiar friendship and kindness with which he has always honored me, has been pleased to call this tree [Mountain Laurel]… *Kalmia latifolia*."

Thick leaves with curled-under edges help save water.

Bog Rosemary

8 to 18 inches

Bog Laurel

8 to 18 inches

Lethal Little Lovely

Careless cattle, horses, sheep and goats have died from grazing Bog Laurel. High concentrations of an andromedotoxin (diterpene) and a glycoside known as arbutin are to blame.

Of more interest to non-ranching people, is the fact that both toxic substances are released when plant parts are boiled in water, as when making tea. Several people have been poisoned, resulting in symptoms of slowed pulse, lowered blood pressure, nausea, vomiting, convulsions, vertigo, blindness and progressive paralysis, which left untreated could possibly lead to death. I'm happy to report that no confirmed deaths of humans have occurred.

May	June	July

Labrador Tea
Ledum groenlandicum

Bog-loving Labrador Tea is a member of the Ericaceae, the Heath family. It was well known to the Ojibwa people as *muskeegobug aniibi*, or "swamp-growing tea" (note that our word "muskeg" comes from the Ojibwa language). Similarly, the closely related Cree call it

"Hairy arm-pits" help Labrador Tea conserve precious moisture.

muskeko-pukwan. Some folks know it as St. James tea, Hudson's Bay tea, Indian tea, swamp tea and country tea. Thoreau thought the plant's odor was somewhere "between turpentine and strawberries." Okaaaay.

Moose and Woodland Caribou are said to munch on the stems, though another source says animals do not partake since it is slightly poisonous. Keep your eyes open and check for yourself.

Its range extends from Alaska east to Greenland and across the northern tier of states. Labrador Tea is associated with wet Black Spruce swamps and any acidic site with subsurface water, shaded or sunny.

Hairy Armpits

Leathery tops, curled-under edges and fuzzy undersides are leaf traits that help reduce water loss in bog plants—very important attributes if you need to survive in a harsh environment where winter winds steal moisture and your roots can be locked in ice for six months each year.

Tea Totaling

Tea has long been the preferred trail drink for native peoples. *Neebeeshaubo* ("tea") to the Ojibwa meant Labrador Tea. In 1743, a factor at Fort York on Hudson Bay, James Isham, claims that his nervous disorder was cured by "constant drinking one pint [of tea] made strong, for three months." But when

Labrador Tea sprouts from rhizomes following forest fires.

May	June	July

12 to 36 inches

making tea, it is best to steep the leaves in hot water. Do not boil! Boiling releases andromedotoxins, which if drunk in quantity can cause all kinds of side effects. The more northerly *Ledum glandulosum* is likely more poisonous than our species. Are the poisonous traits of *L. groenlandicum* exaggerated?

Red Man's Red Man®

The Baffin Island Inuit used the stems as a chewing tobacco. Other native peoples sucked the leaves and put the astringent mash on burns. The Dene people of Canada used the tea to help them sleep. Hoarse and coughing settlers made a syrup from the tea to ease their symptoms. Modern herbalist sources say it stimulates nerves and the stomach, is very high in vitamin C and it is a treatment for flu, cough, diabetes and high blood pressure. As of this writing, whole Labrador Tea leaves were selling for $11 per pound on Internet herbal medicine sites.

Ghost Buster!

A closely-related species, *Ledum palustre,* in Scandinavian Lapland, was used by the Sami people to keep rodents away from stored grain. It was tied in bundles and placed in the granaries. In Russia, the leaves were used to keep things other than rodents away…ghosts! A more mundane Russian use was in the tanning of leather.

A Real Rhododendron?

Recent studies of *Ledum groenlandicum* DNA suggest it may indeed be a rhododendron according to the Royal British Columbia Museum, but the results are controversial and not widely accepted. It certainly resembles a mini-rhododendron now that they mention it.

Leatherleaf
Chamaedaphne calyculata

Widespread around the northern crown of the globe, Leatherleaf is found in nearly every boggy situation: Black Spruce muskeg, bog pond margins, sedge fens; anywhere the pH is below 5.0. Leatherleaf is the major component of the habitat class known as the "scrub-shrub wetland."

Wind and jarring shake the tiny seeds from their dried box-like capsule.

Winter seeds are an important food source for northern Ruffed Grouse.

Rolled leaf margins increase the protective shell of air (boundary layer) around the leaf, creating more resistance to vapor diffusion.

Leatherleaf is a dominant bog shrub that can survive fire due to its deep submerged roots. It is the first shrub to get a foothold in newly established boggy Sphagnum Moss beds.

Bumblebees fertilize Leatherleaf. The bushes are able to self-fertilize but in the long run they would suffer from much lower seed production and less genetic variation.

Evergreen leaves save the plant energy; Leatherleaf doesn't have to grow new ones in the spring.

24 to 48 inches

May	June	July

Cotton-Grass
Eriophorum species

Cotton-grass is not a grass; it is a sedge. Sedges have triangular stems in cross section. Remember the saying, "sedges have edges." Just as we use the name Kleenex® for several brands of tissue, cotton-grass is the generic name for seven species of acid-loving sedges in our North Woods.

Eriophorum has its roots in the Greek *erion* or "wool" and *phoros* meaning "bearing" referring to its cotton-like flower head.

10 to 20 inches

Cotton-grass is neither cotton nor a grass; it is a sedge.

| May | June | July |

Relatives of our cotton-grasses grow profusely in Scandinavia, Germany and the Snowdonia region of Wales.

Stable Sedge

Nearly all cotton-grasses grow in climax spruce-fir bogs of the North. This stable environment will continue on indefinitely unless fire or forest encroachment alters the status quo. Tawny Cotton-Grass (*Eriophorum virginicum*), for example, grows from mounds called tussocks, which can represent 50 years of growth.

Research by McGraw, Vavrek and Bennington found that seeds of Sheathed Cotton-Grass (*Eriophorum vaginatum*) unearthed near Eagle Creek, Alaska were viable after an estimated 200 years!

Redpoll Snack

Common Redpolls in New Brunswick feed on Tawny Cotton-Grass seed-heads sticking up out of the snow.

Lampwicking

For centuries the Inuit people of the High Arctic have used the wool of cotton-grass (*quliq*) for wicks in their stone oil-lamps.

LAKES,

Marshes, ponds and some lakes are very productive environments. Decaying vegetation is rapidly recycled into mineral nutrients and soluble organic compounds by a parade of decomposers—bacteria, worms and aquatic insects. This frees up the resources needed for new plant growth and animal production. Wetlands are far more productive than most forests.

Lake vegetation can vary dramatically depending on water movement, bottom substrate and water hardness. The plants included here are found in deep marshes or vegetated shorelines where the water is six inches to 36 inches deep. You'll find a whole different group of plants in a nutrient-rich clay-and-muck-bottomed lake (mesotrophic or eutrophic) versus a clear nutrient-poor granite-bound lake (oligotrophic).

Don't confuse a marsh with a swamp. Marshes are sunny areas of shallow water dominated by cattails and

MARSHES & PONDS
Wet Shorelines & Open Water

rushes. No Sphagnum Mosses are present. Swamps are in wooded areas, often under Black Ash or Northern White Cedar.

Bucky the Maintenance Rodent
The world's second largest rodent, the Beaver, is solely responsible for maintaining thousands of ponds in the North Woods. Their dams along moving waterways create havens, not only for themselves, but for trout, frogs, Moose and aquatic plants.

Salty Treat
Water-lilies are a critical component of the pond flora. Moose can't get enough of them. Why this obsession? Simple. Moose crave salt and research has shown that water-lilies and other aquatic plants are 10 to 400-times higher in sodium than the twigs and needles Moose browse in winter. Aquatic plants in healthy, non-stagnant ponds and lakes concentrate sodium and other minerals.

And like their plant-eating buddies, Moose find it hard to get enough salt into their diet. These half-ton herbivores will even dive down to 18 feet to access aquatic munchies like water-lily.

Marsh Skullcap
Scutellaria galericulata

Hidden among the sedges and wetland grasses are the paired purple flowers of Marsh Skullcap. The flower's sloping front-edge is actually fused petals that resemble a monk's skullcap.

It's Hip to be Square
Marsh Skullcap is a true mint (family Lamiaceae) and like all mints, it has a square stem. Feel for yourself.

Though skullcap does not smell, it is related to some famous aromatic mints: basil, thyme, oregano and peppermint.

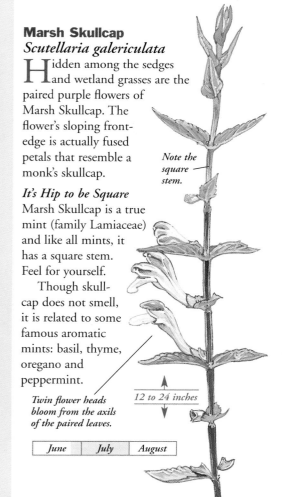

Note the square stem.

Twin flower heads bloom from the axils of the paired leaves.

12 to 24 inches

| June | July | August |

Swamp Milkweed
Asclepias incarnata

Old Beaver meadows, wet ditches and marshy shorelines are the places one is likely to find this tall milkweed. The showy pink flowers are clustered in a rounded head. They do not bloom all at once but rather in bunches, attracting a myriad of bees and flies who crave the copious nectar they produce.

The literal translation of the Latin name is "flesh of the pink northern Europeans." That's funny. Other less insulting names include swamp silkweed, rose silkweed, water nerveroot, flesh-colored silkweed and white Indian-hemp.

Indian Hemp
Howard Stansbury, the leader of an expedition to Utah in 1850, found Swamp Milkweed growing around springs near the Great Salt Lake. He said the Pueblo Indians "cut it down when ripe, rub it so as to separate the fibers, and make of it beautiful and very strong fishing lines and fine sewing thread."

Milkweed Beetles and Monarchs
Like other milkweeds, the milky sap of this species contains a glycoside that is poisonous to most critters. Monarch Butterfly caterpillars, milkweed beetles (*Tetraopes* species) and milkweed bugs (*Oncopeltus* species) are the exception, as they are able to eat the plant and remain unaffected. Their little insect-bodies even retain enough of the poison to make themselves unpalatable to other predators.

Swamp Chew
By placing the milky sap near a fire to coagulate, some tribes made an acceptable chewing gum.

June	July	August

Botanists label Swamp Milkweed a "high reward" flower. Its copious nectar is craved by summer insects.

24 to 48 inches

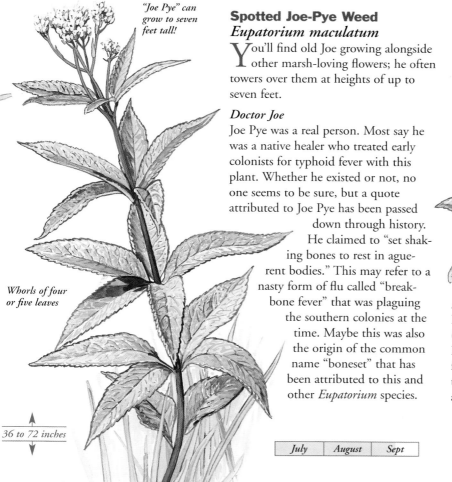

"Joe Pye" can grow to seven feet tall!

Whorls of four or five leaves

36 to 72 inches

Spotted Joe-Pye Weed
Eupatorium maculatum

You'll find old Joe growing alongside other marsh-loving flowers; he often towers over them at heights of up to seven feet.

Doctor Joe

Joe Pye was a real person. Most say he was a native healer who treated early colonists for typhoid fever with this plant. Whether he existed or not, no one seems to be sure, but a quote attributed to Joe Pye has been passed down through history. He claimed to "set shaking bones to rest in ague-rent bodies." This may refer to a nasty form of flu called "break-bone fever" that was plaguing the southern colonies at the time. Maybe this was also the origin of the common name "boneset" that has been attributed to this and other *Eupatorium* species.

| July | August | Sept |

Individual flowers don't open all at once. Some are in bloom while others are still in the bud stage.

Royal Honor

King Eupator of Parthia (120-63 B.C.) was one of Rome's most belligerent foes. He was credited with discovering the medicinal uses of these plants that are now named after him—*Eupatorium*.

Marsh Cinquefoil
Potentilla palustris

Maybe we should call Marsh Cinquefoil "Powerful Five-leaved Herb of the Swamp." The genus *Potentilla*, which translates to "potent herb" or "powerful herb" and the species epithet, *palustris*, is Latin for "of the swamp." Cinquefoil literally means "five leaves." In fact, some call it by the name marsh five-finger. *Sumpf blutauge* is German for "swamp blood-eye" and a wonderful vernacular name for this plant. The Norwegians called it *myrhatt* or "bog hat," while the Swedes know it by the colorful name *kråkklover* or "crow clover."

Marshes and bogs around the northern crown of the globe harbor Marsh Cinquefoil; it grows in northern Ireland, Scandinavia, Russia, and in Canada from Hudson Bay south to our beloved North Woods.

The deep burgundy flowers give off a stench that attracts carrion-feeding insects (especially flies) that then serve as pollinators.

Deer and beaver browse Marsh Cinquefoil.

Russian Tea
In Russia, the leaves are used as a substitute for tea. It has also been used for tanning hides and dyeing fabrics a yellow-brown tint.

June	July	August

Marsh St. Johnswort
Triadenum virginicum

A low plant of wet and marshy places, Marsh St. Johnswort is one of the few plants that are easily recognized by their flower buds, which are large and burgundy.

Crepuscular critters (dawn and dusk-active) pollinate this plant so there is no need for the flower to be open during the day. Marsh St. Johnswort protects its pollen source by staying closed during most daylight hours.

8 to 18 inches

Saynt Johannesworte

12 to 18 inches

Throughout history, St. Johnswort species have been seen as protectors. The Latin name for our yellow species is *Hypericum*, a corruption of the Greek *hupereikon* or "above a picture" and refers to the practice of hanging this plant over religious iconic art to ward off the evil presence of witches, goblins and the devil at midsummer festivals. In 1525 Rycharde Banckes wrote, "This is saynt Johannes worte. The vertue of it is thus. If it be put in a mannes house, there shall come no wicked spyryte therein." The Saint John in reference is none other than the proclaimer of Christ, John the Baptist.

| June | July | August |

Wild Iris
Iris versicolor

Proliferating in marshes and along lake margins, bunches of Wild Irises are a brief but stunning addition to summer.

Goddess of the Rainbows

Iris is the goddess of rainbows. As a messenger of the gods, she constantly needed to move between the heavens and earth; the rainbow was her bridge.

French Connection

The familiar *fleur-de-lis*, the symbol of French nobility, is also found on the flag of Duluth, Minnesota. Why? The French explorer, Daniel Greysolon Sieur DuLhut, was the first white explorer to set foot on the sands of Duluth's shore.

The literal translation of *fleur-de-lis* is "flower of lily" but some believe its origins were as the "flower of Louis,"—King Louis VII, that is, the first to use the symbol on his shield. Others contend that it is possibly a corruption of *fleur de la Lys*, a river in Flanders where irises grow in great profusion.

Snake Charmer

The Ojibwa would take a bit of Wild Iris with them while blueberry picking to keep snakes away.

24 to 36 inches

Sword-like leaves are diagnostic, even when not in bloom.

Bees pollinate irises. After gallivanting among other irises, a pollen-dusted bee may crawl up the "yellow brick road" that forms on the iris's colorful lower petal. As it tries to bully its way in to the nectar source, pollen from its back is brushed onto the flower's pistil, thereby accomplishing pollination.

| May | June | July |

Tufted Loosestrife
Lysimachia thyrsiflora

Wet lake margins are home to this species of *Lysimachia,* which sports paired "tufts" of yellow flowers. Tufted Loosestrife is a circumboreal species that is only found as far south as Colorado, Nebraska and New Jersey. It is widespread in northern North America and Scandinavia and grows east to Central Europe and Russia.

Like Fringed Loosestrife and Swamp Candles, Tufted Loosestrife is a member of the Primrose family (*Primulaceae*) and not a real loosestrife at all. The invasive alien, Purple Loosestrife (*Lythrum salicaria*), is a member of the true Loosestrife family (*Lythraceae*).

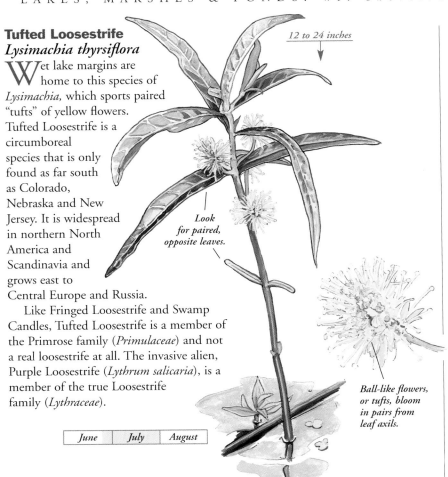

12 to 24 inches

Look for paired, opposite leaves.

Ball-like flowers, or tufts, bloom in pairs from leaf axils.

June	July	August

Swamp Candles
Lysimachia terrestris

A bright yellow spike of delicate four-petaled flowers shines from the company of sedges and grasses along wet lake edges. I love the name "Swamp Candles," but others have known it as bog loosestrife or yellow loosestrife — not to be confused with the Yellow Loosestrife of Europe (*Lysimachia vulgaris*).

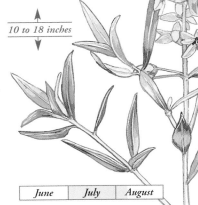

10 to 18 inches

June	July	August

A canoe may be the best way to find these three Lysimachia species.

Fringed Loosestrife
Lysimachia ciliata

New World Yellow Loosestrife

The first North American written account of this species, or one of its yellow cousins, was by John Josselyn in 1638 who wrote of a "yellow *Lysimachus* of Virginia." What an amazing experience to be one of the first to describe the exotic flowers of a "brand new" continent. Of course, the Indians already knew the local flora intimately.

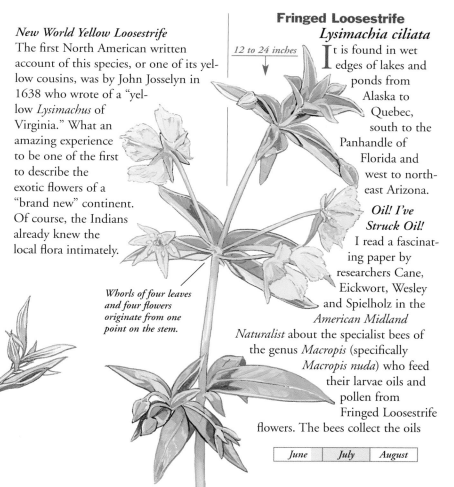

12 to 24 inches

Whorls of four leaves and four flowers originate from one point on the stem.

It is found in wet edges of lakes and ponds from Alaska to Quebec, south to the Panhandle of Florida and west to northeast Arizona.

Oil! I've Struck Oil!

I read a fascinating paper by researchers Cane, Eickwort, Wesley and Spielholz in the *American Midland Naturalist* about the specialist bees of the genus *Macropis* (specifically *Macropis nuda*) who feed their larvae oils and pollen from Fringed Loosestrife flowers. The bees collect the oils

| June | July | August |

from trichome (gland-bearing) hairs on the flowers, mix it with pollen and roll the mixture into tiny balls which are taken back to their underground nests that are lined with water-resistant chemicals. Purportedly this is the only New World example of mutualism between an oil-collecting bee and an oil-bearing flower outside of the tropics.

Coincidently, in the fens of England, two cousins to our bee and flower have a similar relationship. *Macropis europaea*, "a bee rather smaller than a honeybee," gets oil from Yellow Loosestrife (*Lysimachia vulgaris*). The *Lysimachias* are one of several unrelated genera scattered across the globe that present oil instead of nectar to the specialized bees that visit them.

A Lot of Bull!

Genus *Lysimachia* is named after King Lysimachos of Thrace (360-281 B.C.), who is said to have tamed a wild bull with a stalk of loosestrife. Sounds like a lot of bull to me.

Pickerelweed
Pontederia cordata

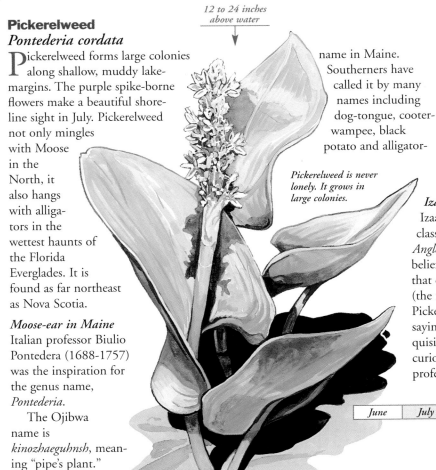

12 to 24 inches
above water

Pickerelweed forms large colonies along shallow, muddy lake-margins. The purple spike-borne flowers make a beautiful shoreline sight in July. Pickerelweed not only mingles with Moose in the North, it also hangs with alligators in the wettest haunts of the Florida Everglades. It is found as far northeast as Nova Scotia.

Moose-ear in Maine
Italian professor Biulio Pontedera (1688-1757) was the inspiration for the genus name, *Pontederia*.

The Ojibwa name is *kinozhaeguhnsh*, meaning "pipe's plant." Moose-ear is a folk name in Maine. Southerners have called it by many names including dog-tongue, cooter-wampee, black potato and alligator-

Pickerelweed is never lonely. It grows in large colonies.

wampee. The name wampee is borrowed from an Indian name for the plant, *wampi*.

Red Sticky Fruit on a Stick
Ducks and other animals eat the red berries. Each berry contains one starchy seed. These seeds can be eaten raw like nuts, dried or ground into flour. The leaves may be cooked.

Izaak Punts
Izaak Walton in his 1676 classic, *The Compleat Angler*, relates the bizarre belief by some in England that certain Northern Pike (the fish) are bred from Pickerelweed. Izaak deferred, saying, "I shall leave to the disquisitions of men of more curiosity and leisure than I profess myself to have."

| June | July | August |

3 to 10 inches
above water

Wild Calla
Calla palustris

Large clusters of these white-hooded water-dwellers inhabit the stagnant pools of ditches, swamps and lakes, their heart-shaped leaves over-shadow the flow-ers. *Calla* is believed to come from the Greek word *kalos* that means "beauti-ful." *Calla palustris* translates to "beauty of the marsh." Other names include water arum, female-dragon, water-dragon and swamp-robin.

Just like Jack

The Wild Calla flower is actually a spathe-spadix combination similar to that found in Jack-in-the-Pulpit. The white spathe (like Jack's "pulpit") that forms a hood over the spadix (like Jack himself) is actu-ally a modified flower bract. The spadix hosts the flowers that ripen into glossy red berries later in the summer.

Wild Calla's "white cape" is called the spathe and is actually a modified flower bract.

May	June	July

A terrestrial form of Water Smartweed grows on dry land and has erect leaves.

Water Smartweed
Polygonum amphibium

"Stunning" is the only word for large colonies of Water Smartweed in mucky backwater shal-lows. Hundreds of pink thumb-sized flower spikes peek above their own floating leaves, creating a sea of fuchsia. It is hard to believe this gorgeous flower is related to its vacant-lot "white trash" cousins, Black Bindweed and Knotweed.

Large colonies of Water Smartweed with hundreds of flowers can be found in backwater bays.

June	July	August

2 to 5 inches above water

Broad-leaved Arrowhead or Duck Potato
Sagittaria latifolia

Both common names for this muck-lover are apropos; the broad arrow-head-shaped leaves are as distinctive to flower-peekers as the swollen, underwater tubers are to dabbling ducks, gobbling geese and submerged swans. Crinkle-petaled white flowers radiate by threes from the flower stalk. To get a close look at arrowhead you'll get your moccasins mucky.

Poor Little Muskrats

Muskrats, swans, ducks and native peoples all depended on the small round potato-like Arrowhead tubers for sustenance. Tribes across the continent, from the Cherokee in the southeast to the Thompson Indians of British

Columbia, and the Poma of California to the Ojibwa of the Great Lakes, made "duck potatoes" a food staple, eating them either roasted or boiled. The Meskwaki Indians of Iowa got smart and let the Muskrats do the wet work of collecting the tubers. The Meskwaki would then steal the little round prizes from the Muskrat houses. Yes, sad but true. Poor little Muskrats.

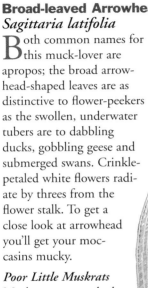

Broad-leaved Arrowhead leaves can be wide or narrow.

6 to 12 inches above water

| June | July | August |

Water Hemlock
Cicuta maculata

Steer clear of this tall aquatic member of the carrot family if you have munching on your mind. It is extremely poisonous

Socratic Suicide

Socrates was ordered to commit suicide in 399 B.C. by drinking a tea of Poison Hemlock (*Conium maculatum*), a close European cousin of Water Hemlock. This was considered the "humane" method of execution at the time.

Water Hemlock is one of the most poisonous plants in the United States.

Most folks who've died from water hemlock have mistaken it for Water Parsnip (*Sium suave*).

Note that the stem of this poisonous plant is smooth while that of the non-poisonous Water Parsnip is corrugated.

36 to 72 inches

Both plants are members of the Carrot (or Parsley) family: the Umbelliferae. The poison is cicutoxin, which directly affects the central nervous system causing violent convulsions a mere 15 to 20 minutes after ingestion.

Moreau's Carrot

The voyageurs called Water Hemlock, *carotte de Moreau*, or "Moreau's carrot," after the demise of one of their fellow canoe men who mistakenly partook of this plant.

June	July	August

Water Shield
Brasenia schreberi

You'll probably first notice the dense matte of floating football-shaped leaves on mud-bottomed northern lakes long before the small purple flowers catch your eye. The leaves are smaller than those of the Bullhead Lily and Fragrant White Water-Lily.

In America it is also known as water-jelly, deerfood, egg-bonnet, frogleaf, little water-lily, purple-dock and purple-bonnet. Water Shield is wide-ranging, it is found from the North Woods to Europe, Asia, Africa and Australia.

The Master's Student

The specific epithet, *schreberi*, is named for German botanist Johann Christian Daniel Schreber (1739-1810), a student of Linnaeus's in Uppsala, Sweden.

Slimy Salad

According to former Quetico naturalist Shan Walshe, the stems and young leaves of Water Shield may be "eaten raw in a salad, slime and all."

Unlike the big gaudy flowers of White Water-Lily, the blossoms of Water Shield are small and easily overlooked.

June	July	August

Common White Water-Lily & Fragrant White Water-Lily
Nymphaea tuberosa & Nymphaea odorata

These two species are, for our purposes, basically the same. Sure, one smells more than the other does, but most of us would tip our canoe trying to get a whiff anyway.

Toad lily, pond lily, water-queen, water-nymph, beaver-root, alligator-bonnet, cow-cabbage and fairy-boats are just a few of its colorful names.

Leaf length 6 to 12 inches

Rafts of water-lily leaves shade the pond's bottom, effectively cutting off sunlight and eliminating potential competition.

Pure of Heart

Thoreau's journal for June 26, 1852 observes, "the *Nymphaea odorata*, water nymph, sweet water lily, pond-lily, in bloom. A superb flower, our lotus queen of the waters. How sweet, innocent, wholesome its fragrance. How pure its white petals, though its root is in the mud!"

A Cure for Baldness?

To Ojibwa men, their hair was their glory: long, black and silky. Baldness was a serious blow to their manhood. (Some things never change.) This may be the reason one finds several cures for hair loss in the literature of Native American ethnobotany. The root of this plant, in fact, was thought to slow the natural process of hair loss.

Sunny, warm days are when the flowers really open up. They stay closed in cool temps.

| June | July | August |

Bullhead Lily
Nuphar luteum (N. variegatum)

Bullhead Lilies grow from the muddy shallows of our summer lakes; their flower heads stand up just above the surface of the water like so many teed-up yellow golf balls. The flowers never open wide as they do in White Water-Lilies.

Spatterdock, yellow pond lily, beaver lily, cow lily, dog lily, flatterdock (England), frog lily, Indian pond lily and yellow-lanterns are just a few of the vernacular names.

Cross-pollination Guaranteed!

When the Bullhead Lily's yellow blossom is still tightly balled, the only passage in to the flower is a tiny triangular opening over the stigma. As a bee squeezes its way in, it is forced past the stigma. The next day the flower opens wider, revealing the pollen-laden anthers and allowing access to other bees thereby assuring cross-pollination.

Popcorn, Potatoes and Porridge

Rootstalks of Bullhead Lilies may be boiled like potatoes, but be sure and use several changes of water. The seeds can be dried and ground into flour or heated in oil and popped like popcorn. Klamath Indians, reported Frederick Coville in 1897, "gather enormous quantities of it during the months of July and August, nearly all the old women of the tribe going to the marsh for the purpose." He went on to say that they either fried and popped the dried seeds or ground them into meal for bread or porridge.

Hungry Moose Beware

As anyone who has spent much time in the Boundary Waters knows, Moose love water lilies. This was reported as early as 1672 by John Josselyn who wrote, "The Moose deer feed much upon them, at which time the Indians kill them, when their heads are under water."

In addition to these Bullhead lillies there is also a variety with a red disk appropriately called Red-disked Bullhead Lily.

Muskrat Love...Tubers

The Ojibwa roasted and ate the large rootstalk. To gather this staple they often raided the caches of the local Muskrats that had stashed the tubers of water lilies and arrowhead plants in their houses for winter use.

| June | July | August |

Home, Sweet Home

Developing *Water-Lily Beetles* (Galerucella nymphaeae) *depend on the floating leaves of* Nuphar lutea *for their very existence. In late May and early June, dozens of eggs are laid on the leaf tops. The young eat their "home, sweet home," creating scars that allow bacteria and fungi to attack the leaf.*

The decomposing leaf sinks and the beetles abandon ship. Unfortunately, they cannot swim and must float around in the hopes of connecting with another Bullhead Lily leaf where they will become an adult.

White Water-Lilies also host dependent beetles. The metallic-purple Donacia *beetles can be seen gathering pollen in the flower on sunny summer days.*

THE SUMMER FOREST
Deep Shade & Sunny Edges

The "summer forest" is a generic term for several forest types in the North Woods: northern hardwoods, aspen stands, pure maple woods and mixed coniferous-deciduous forests. What they have in common are more neutral to alkaline soils (mull humus) than those found in acidic bogs and boreal forests (mor humus).

Mull humus is a calcium-rich, well-mixed loam that has plenty of bacteria to capture nitrogen from the atmosphere and make it available to green plants. The "recycling crew" is a healthy mix of earthworms, slugs, millipedes, insect larvae, bacteria and fungi.

Mull this Over
Leaf litter composition plays a major role in determining soil pH. Needles of spruce, fir and pine make for acidic humus while maple, basswood and alder leaves have a low carbon to nitrogen ratio, which allows them to be easily decomposed. If we look at a cross-section of the leaf litter in the mull humus of a summer forest from the top down, we'd find:

- Dry, intact leaves with no insect damage.
- Limp leaves that are damp.
- "Holy" leaves chewed by mites and other insects.
- Dark leaves are still recognizable but with a slimy layer of microorganisms.
- Skeletonized leaves with only the petiole and veins intact.
- White fungal roots (mycorrhizae) cover what's left of the leaves.
- Only bits and pieces of leaves remain.
- Finally, the decomposed organic material that forms soils.

Soils 101: The Recyclers
The textbook definition of soil is "the transition between complex organic matter of formerly living things and simple elemental inorganic material."

But how does the organic matter locked up in leaves, tree stumps and dead animals get converted to inorganic material? Decomposition is the answer. This process takes the complex carbohydrates and proteins and converts them to basic atoms.

The key players in the recycling program are bacteria, fungi, earthworms, springtails, mites, slugs, millipedes, carrion beetles, carpenter ants, sowbugs and insect larvae. Ninety percent of the total weight of forest plants is broken down by these agents of decomposition.

Rich soils in the summer forest create ideal growing conditions for shade-tolerant plants. Others seek sunny woodland edges.

Wild Columbine
Aquilegia canadensis

Columbine is the eye-candy of the wildflower world. Who can resist the red and yellow blossoms? They grow from rocky clefts in sun-dappled light or gravelly edges in full sun. I prefer the subtle nature of our wild columbine to the larger-flowered domestic variety.

Jesters, Doves and Gloves

One source describes the flower as "five doves standing in a circle." This would explain the Latin root, *columba* meaning "dove." I questioned this description at first, but now I can see it—five crimson-colored doves facing each other in a circle, wings partially spread. Honestly, though, I prefer to think of the Wild Columbine flower as a jester's hat. The French Canadians call this plant *gants de Notre Dame*— the "gloves of Notre Dame." Sure, why not?

Everybody Wants a Little Sugar

Tiny bulbous nectaries are found in the modified petals at the tip of the flowers. They are too deep for bumblebees (*Bombus* species) to get at, but halictid bees (*Halictus* species) and honeybees (*Apis* species) gather pollen, ensuring cross-fertilization. Butterflies and moths attempt the awkward upside-down maneuver to get their proboscis up to the nectar but are rarely successful. Hummingbirds are very adept at accessing the nectaries with their long retractable tongue.

Love Potion Number 'bine

It was the belief of a certain Native American tribe (probably the Pawnee) that a suitor who dusted his palm with powdered columbine seeds and held the hand of the woman he was wooing, would win her heart and live happily ever after.

Columbine Cologne

The Natives of the Missouri River region, especially the Omaha and Ponca, used the crushed columbine seeds to make an irresistible cologne. Indian men of nearly every North American tribe were known to be quite concerned with their looks and odor. The Omaha chewed the seed to a mash and applied it to their clothing. The odor lasted a long time and was renewed when dampened by rain.

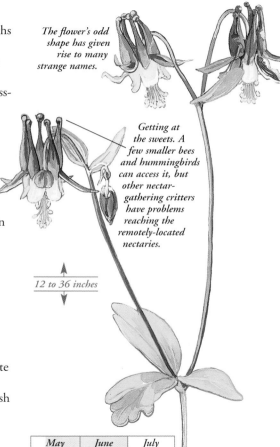

The flower's odd shape has given rise to many strange names.

Getting at the sweets. A few smaller bees and hummingbirds can access it, but other nectar-gathering critters have problems reaching the remotely-located nectaries.

12 to 36 inches

| May | June | July |

Jack-in-the-Pulpit
Arisaema triphyllum

Jack-in-the-Pulpit is a member of the Dragon Arum family—a large, mostly tropical group that includes the houseplants philodendron and caladium.

With such a unique physical presence, it is no surprise that Jack has many aliases: Indian-turnip, Adam's-apple, brown-dragon, cuckoo plant, devil's-ear, parson-in-the-pulpit, Indian-cradle and thrice-leaved arum are just a few.

Pollinating insects are attracted to Jack's B.O., which has been likened to the odor of a stagnant pool.

The amount of color in the "pulpit" is dependent on the amount of sunlight reaching it; the purpler the pulpit, the more shaded the site. Is this really true? Observe for yourself.

Sex change for Jack?
Jack-in-the-Pulpit grows from an underground corm of stored nutrients. The amount of nutrients stored in the corm determines the sex of the plant.

But this amount can change from year to year. Nutrient-rich soils produce large corms, which, in turn, produce female flowers (pistillate) while male flowers (with stamens) require fewer nutrients. Very poor soils result in corms that are tiny and may only produce the leaf stalk and no flowers.

Hopi Tablespoons
I read somewhere that the Hopi believed one tablespoon of Jack-in-the-Pulpit extract caused temporary sterility while two tablespoons made it a permanent condition. I hope they measured carefully. By the way, did the early Hopi really have tablespoons?

Indian Turnip
The starch-rich underground corm was known to early settlers as the "Indian turnip" and is edible if boiled in several changes of water.

"Jack" is actually a fleshy spike known to botanists as the spadix. Tiny flowers cover Jack's lower half.

His pulpit is the leaf-like spathe.

12 to 24 inches

Starches stored in the underground corm give Jack a headstart at spring's growth spurt.

Look carefully! J often hiding unde canopy of his own

| May | June | July |

Wild Sarsaparilla
Aralia nudicaulis

Walk any wild path in early summer and you're likely to see this showy plant. The large three-branched leaves overshadow the lower flower stalk that appears to spring from the ground on an entirely separate stem.

Root Beer's Roots

Legend has it that in the early 1900s a drink made from the root of this plant was introduced into the logging camps of the North Woods. The lumberjacks soundly rejected the new drink called sarsaparilla (SAS-pa-rill-a). In a clever marketing move, the salesmen changed the name of their delicious drink to "root beer" and, lo and behold, the frothy refreshment became popular with

the rough-edged lumbermen. Later on, *Smilax officinalis*, a native plant of Honduras, became the "real" sarsaparilla used in early root beer manufacturing.

Horse Rub and Fish Charm

Is your horse exhausted and about ready to drop? Early native peoples would rub Wild Sarsaparilla root, steeped with other herbs, on the horse's chest and legs to rejuvenate the tired beast. Eastern Canada's Montagnais Indians formerly fermented the purple berries to make a wine for use as a health tonic. The Ojibwa once believed that rubbing their nets with a mixture of Wild Sarsaparilla root and Sweet Flag (*Acorus calamus*) was effective in luring fish.

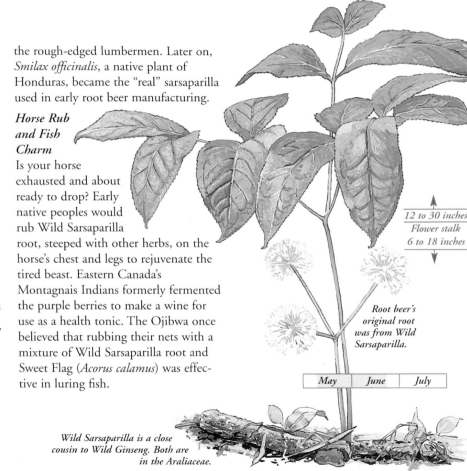

12 to 30 inches
Flower stalk
6 to 18 inches

Root beer's original root was from Wild Sarsaparilla.

| May | June | July |

Flower clusters are three perfectly-round ball-like heads of tiny green flowers.

Detail of a single flower.

Wild Sarsaparilla is a close cousin to Wild Ginseng. Both are in the Araliaceae.

Spotted Touch-me-not or Jewelweed
Impatiens capensis

This tall sun-loving plant can bear dozens of flowers…spotted orange jewels in the shape of a horn-of-plenty.

Old folk-names include Jack-jump-up-and-kiss-me (Newfoundland), eardrop, ear-jewel, horns-of-plenty, kicking-colt, lady's-eardrop, snapweed, weathercock and speckled-jewels.

Don't Scratch Your Itch
Got a rash from Poison Ivy or Stinging Nettles? Try rubbing Jewelweed leaves on the itchy spot for instant relief. It works! American Indians knew this trick long before passing on the dermatological knowledge to the first settlers. Early ethnobotanical research indicates that the Jewelweed cure was known not only by the local Ojibwa but also the Cherokee, Iroquois, Meskwaki, Mohegan, Nanticoke, Omaha, Penobscot, Potawatomi and Shinnecock—proof that skin-care tips, like trade goods, were spread across the continent in Pre-Columbian times.

Nectaries deep in the curled corolla are only accessible to long-tongued pollinators like bumblebees, sphinx moths and hummingbirds. Some "nectar thieves" cut through the flower to get at the sweet stuff.

24 to 48 inches

Got a bad case of Poison Ivy and no calamine lotion? No problem! Simply rub Jewelweed leaves on the rash for instant relief.

| June | July | August |

Anyone for a Seed Spitting Contest?
Ripe seedpods build up great hydrostatic pressure and explode upon the slightest disturbance, hurling a seed up to five feet! This seed-dispersal method is how we come by the common name, "touch-me-not." Henry David Thoreau commented on this in his manuscript *Wild Fruits*, "Touch-me-not seed vessels, as all know, go off like pistols on the slightest touch, and so suddenly and energetically that they always startle you, though you are expecting it."

He Becomes She
The orange flowers all bloom as males with five exposed anthers. After only one day, all anthers fall off, revealing the female stigma. He has become she. This insures cross-fertilization…or does it?

Look for tiny bud-like structures hanging from leaf axils. These boring flowers do not attract insects or hummingbirds, nor do they need to. They self-fertilize. It is an effective backup to insect pollination.

Rose Twisted-Stalk
Streptopus roseus

Mixed deciduous-coniferous forests with acid soils are the preferred home for this North Woods lily.

The Greek *streptopus* means "bent or twisted stem" and refers to the way the stalk zigs and zags at every leaf attachment point. Rosy bells hang from these same intersections, eventually ripening into translucent red berries. As with all members of the Lily family, the leaves have parallel venation and flower parts are in multiples of three. False Solomon's Seal (*Smilacina racemosa*) also has narrow parallel-veined leaves but its flower and fruits are borne at the tip of the stalk, not in the leaf axils. Hairy Solomon's Seal (*Polygonatum pubescens*) has two bell-like flowers hanging from each leaf axil.

The Trots by Any Other Name

The shiny red berries look so tempting, just hanging there, waiting to be picked. But wait. One of the plant's nicknames is scootberry. This quote from Sylvanus

12 to 24 inches

Hayward in 1891 explains; "*Streptopus roseus* I learned to call scootberry long before I understood why it was so called. The sweetish berries were quite eagerly eaten by boys, always acting as a physic, and as the diarrhea was locally called "the scoots," the plant at once received the name."

A delicate rose-colored bell hangs from each leaf axil.

May	June	July

Note how the stem zigs and zags at each leaf attachment point.

Red Baneberry
Actaea rubra

Despite its name, Red Baneberry can bear either red or white berries. These are simply two varieties of the same species. Red-berried plants are more common.

Actaea rubra may produce either red or white berries.

12 to 24 inches

May	June	July

Trollbaer in Norway ("troll berry") is a closely related species. Other common names used in America include doll's-eyes, Chinaberry, coralberry, grapewort, poisonberry, necklaceweed, pearlberry, toadroot, white-beads, red cohosh, redberry, white cohosh and whiteberry snakeroot.

No Child's Play

The nickname for the glossy red or white berries with the black spots is "doll's-eyes." But a high concentration of a poisonous cardiac glycoside makes these tempting berries anything but innocent. As few as six berries can cause vomiting, bloody diarrhea and other symptoms leading to paralysis of respiration, i.e. death.

It's not just the berries that are poisonous; the leaves and roots can also cause serious illness. Deaths of children have occurred in Europe from a closely related species, but no fatalities have been recorded in North America. But, as with most poisonous berries, their "icky" taste discourages indiscriminate munching.

Many animals have a strong detoxification system and seek out baneberries. Grazers include White-footed Mice, Red-backed Voles, American Robins, Yellow-bellied Sapsuckers and Ruffed Grouse.

Dewberry or Dwarf Raspberry
Rubus pubescens

If you genetically crossed a raspberry with a strawberry plant, you'd probably get something like *Rubus pubescens*. The three leaflets resemble strawberry leaves, and the fruit is a glob of translucent red dropelets that reminds one of a raspberry. The plant does not part with its fruit easily as the drupelets tenaciously cling to the receptacle. Let's just say the fruit looks better than it tastes.

Fruits are actually clusters of juicy drupelets. Edible but not a choice fruit.

3 to 6 inches

May	June	July

Wood Strawberry & Meadow Strawberry
Fragaria vesca & Fragaria virginiana

There are two common species of strawberries in the North Woods. As members of the Rose family, Wood and Meadow Strawberries have typical Rose family flowers: five green sepals and five white rounded petals surrounding numerous stamens. Strawberries spread by runners (above-ground stems) and can quickly colonize new areas. One researcher found that a single plant spawned 200 others in three years and covered 70-times the original area.

Strawberries are a favorite Scandinavian treat. Families travel to their mountain *hytta* (cabins), to pick the summer fruit. Norwegians call them *jordbaer* or "earth berry." Ojibwa called this important fruit *odeiminidjibik* or "heart berry root."

Strawberry—Nature's Oral Cleanser
The juice of strawberries is known for its ability to whiten teeth, dissolve tartar and remove plaque. Simply rub the juice of fresh berries on your "not-so-pearly-whites" and rinse with warm water mixed with a bit of baking soda. *Fowler's Extract of Wild Strawberry* is available when wild strawberries are not.

Thoreau's Wild Fruit
Henry David Thoreau in *Wild Fruits* puts forth an opinion that many of us would agree with. "I do not think much of strawberries in gardens. Nor in market baskets, nor in quart boxes, raised and sold by your excellent hard-fisted neighbor. It is those little natural beds or patches of them on the dry hillsides that interest me most, though I may get but a handful at first—not weeded or watered or manured by a hired gardener."

April	May	June

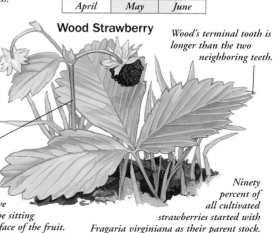

Wood Strawberry

Meadow's terminal tooth is as short, or shorter, than the two neighboring teeth.

3 to 6 inches

Meadow Strawberry has fruits on stems that are shorter than leaves. The berries are rounder and have achenes embedded in pits on the fruit's surface.

Wood's terminal tooth is longer than the two neighboring teeth.

Wood Strawberry has fruits on stems that are taller than leaves. Its berries are more elongated and have achenes that appear to be sitting on the smooth surface of the fruit.

Ninety percent of all cultivated strawberries started with Fragaria virginiana as their parent stock.

Meadow Strawberry

American Red Raspberry
Rubus idaeus

Raspberries are at their full glory in sunny disturbed sites. July is prime picking month, but watch out for the sharp spines on the canes or it will be prime "pricking" month.

24 to 48 inches

Uterine Toner

Modern medicine has finally agreed with a folk remedy that many cultures have known for centuries: raspberry leaf tea eases labor pains by reducing muscle spasms. Fragerine, the chemical found in young raspberry leaves (before the fruit ripens) tones uterine and pelvic muscles. It is most commonly taken as a tea.

The Woodland Cree also used the stem and upper roots to help women recover after childbirth and to slow menstrual bleeding.

May	June	July

Skunk Currant
Ribes glandulosum

Smell the bruised leaves or berries and inhale the strong musk that gives this *Ribes* plant its name. The bristly berries make a great jelly and a decent trail nibble in spite of their odor. The stems have no prickles or spines and sprout leaves shaped like mini maple leaves. Flower clusters are on vertical stalks. This is the most common currant in the canoe country.

The Skunk Loves Fire

Newly scorched soils make a perfect seedbed for Skunk Currant. They thrive in sunny, slightly wet sites for several years following a forest fire. After five years or so, the canopy begins to close as aspens or pines take over and the Skunk Currant declines in the now shaded environment.

10 to 20 inches

Stems are smooth

Gland-tipped hairs cover Skunk Currant fruits.

May	June	July

Thimbleberry
Rubus parviflorus

Thimbleberry is a waist-high bush with huge maple-like leaves and large, flimsy five-petaled white flowers. Deep red fruits develop in August. The soft raspberry-like berries can easily fit over the end of your finger like a thimble. Patient pickers can pluck enough of the tart berries to make excellent pies or jam.

Western Disjunct

The main range of Thimbleberry is the American West, from Alaska to northern Mexico. Our population hugs the shore of Lake Superior and northern Lake Michigan. It is a true western disjunct, separated from its main range by hundreds of miles.

Wasp Condos

Lumpy, peanut-sized growths on Thimbleberry stems are actually galls; they are the result of a tiny, $1/4$-inch-long Cynipid wasp (*Diastrophus kincaidii*).

She lays her eggs in the stem, and the plant responds to the disturbance by growing a mass of tissue around the undeveloped wasps. Dozens of developing young overwinter in the safety of the gall. The adult wasps emerge in the spring.

May	June	July

24 to 48 inches

EXPOSED BEDROCK
Sunny Slabs

"Sharing the stillness of the unimpassioned rock, they also share its endurance."
—*John Ruskin*

Freddy Fungus & Alice Algae

Scandinavians *know* bare stone. Carl Linnaeus, the legendary Swedish botanist, described rock colonization in great detail. He wrote, "the smallest crustaceous lichens begin to cover these arid rocks…. These lichens in time become converted by decay into a thin layer of humus, so that foliose lichens are able to thrust their hyphae into it."

Lichens are actually two plants living together as one. Maybe you've heard of Freddy Fungus and Alice Algae who took a "lichen" to each other and live together in "sin-byosis." But I hear their marriage is on the rocks. Within this "marriage," the fungal partner secretes acids that help dissolve the rock.

Slowly but surely, splatters of lichen mats grow and glean the ingredients of soil: wind-carried dust, mud from rain and decomposing debris. Moss and fern spores ride the wind, gaining a foothold on the shoulders of the crustose lichens. As these new plants die and decay, more soil is built. Finally the neighborhood is "good enough" for herbaceous plants such as the ones in this chapter.

Some forest bedrock openings are carpeted with the branched lichen called Reindeer Moss (*Cladonia rangiferina*). This lichen is crunchy when dry and cushy when saturated with absorbed rain.

But the sunny slab is a temporary condition following fire, wind storms and glaciers. Soon enough, trees encroach, shading out the sun-loving plants. Because of this habitat's impermanence, several plants have seeds that remain viable for decades. Pale Corydalis, Pin Cherry and Bicknell's Geranium are three that employ this survival strategy.

Pale Corydalis
Corydalis sempervirens

A gorgeous sun-lover of rock outcrops in the North Woods, Pale Corydalis has odd pink and yellow flowers that are pollinated by wind and possibly aided by ants. The leaves and stems are a subtle shade of pale green.

Its range runs from Alaska to the northern Rockies of Montana, and from north-central Minnesota to the Appalachians and even up to Newfoundland. In the mountains of Georgia, where it is found on rocky summits, its status is "critically imperiled."

Pale Corydalis can bloom when just three or four inches tall and can grow to two feet or more.

Folk names for Pale Corydalis include rock harlequin, pink-and-yellow corydalis and pink corydalis. *Corydalis* is Greek for "crested lark," possibly referring to the flower's shape.

Essential Essences

I stumbled on a website called alaskanessences.com. They use flowers to develop "essences" that are used "in a variety of therapeutic situations around the world." Though I'm still not sure what an essence is, they say that the Pale Corydalis essence "balances addictive and conditional patterns of loving, helps us see our relationships as catalysts for spiritual growth."

Fire Follower

Pale Corydalis is most common after wildfires on sun-baked bedrock slabs. Why? Old corydalis seeds from decades earlier are able to remain viable in cracks in the rock until a fire opens up the canopy and releases nutrients into the warmed soil. Bicknell's Geranium (*Geranium bicknellii*) and Pin Cherry (*Prunus pensylvanica*) also utilize this long-term survival strategy. Pale Corydalis is a boreal pioneer species that thrives for up to six years following a conflagration. It loves dry sunny sites (don't we all?). Once the canopy closes and the plants are shaded out, they disappear with their future survival riding on the buried seed's ability to germinate following the next fire. Complete fire suppression would spell its demise.

Seeds can survive for decades laying dormant in the soil. Forest fires allow them to germinate.

10 to 24 inches

May	June	July

Bristly Sarsaparilla
Aralia hispida

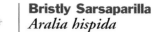

Bristly Sarsaparilla loves to have its feet in granite clefts and its heads in the sun. Look for it on rock slabs exposed to the sun by a recent fire or blowdown. The tiny flowers do not attract much attention, but the blue-black fruits, spaced evenly in round umbels are easy to spot.

Green fruits will ripen to blue-black berries later in the summer.

Algonquin Cure

The Algonquin Indians of Quebec used an infusion of Bristly Sarsaparilla roots to treat heart disease.

12 to 24 inches

June	July	August

Richardson's Alumroot
Heuchera richardsonii

Look for the tall stalks of Alumroot on slabs of slate or granite bedrock, especially in the years following a forest fire. You will find it in the company of Reindeer Moss (*Cladonia rangiferina*), Bristly Sarsaparilla and Pale Corydalis.

The genus *Heuchera* is named for Johan Heinrich Heucher, 1677-1747, a professor of medicine at Wittenberg, Germany. Other common names include cliffweed, cragjangle, mapleleaf, splitrock and rock geranium.

Apos i Poco

Alumroot is a styptic and astringent. A leaf tea has been used for diarrhea, dysentery and piles. Wounds, sores and abrasions are treated with a poultice made from the root. The Blackfeet Indians called a near relative of this plant *apos i poco* and used a concoction of the steeped root to make a healing eye wash. There is even an 1828 claim that it

Alumroot flowers

had "acquired some reputation in the cure of cancer."

Modern Day Meds

Former Canadian Parks naturalist Shan Walshe reported that for relief of sore throat and cough, some Ojibwa on the Lac La Croix Reserve (just north of Minnesota in Canada) still use parts of this plant.

18 to 30 inches

May	June	July

Look for Alumroot on bedrock slabs, especially in the years following a forest fire.

Velvet-leaved Blueberry
Vaccinium myrtilloides

Blueberries are known as *meenum* in the Ojibwa language, "*nummy*" in Sparky-language.

Ojibwa Staple

Blueberries were gathered in great quantities by the Ojibwa and stored for winter use. Along with wild rice, venison, whitefish and maple sugar, blueberries were a true staple of the early Ojibwa.

May	June	July

Nasty, blood-sucking Black Flies pollinate blueberry flowers in May.

Bear Dung Sleuthing

As an astute Canadian naturalist noted, "Bears obviously love blueberries. You only have to see bear dung once during late summer to verify this."

10 to 18 inches

Soft fuzzy leaves are a good clue that you have encountered Velvet-leaved Blueberry.

Bearberry
Arctostaphylos uva-ursi

Bearberry is an evergreen plant of dry, often sandy, soils. Look for big patches of this ground-hugging plant on rock outcrops, ledges and sandy ground beneath pines.

The scientific name for Bearberry is a mixture of Greek (*Arctostaphylos*) and Latin (*uva-ursi*). One means "bear grape" and the other means "grape bear." This begs the question; Do bears eat the berries? The answer is yes.

2 to 5 inches

Kinnikinnik

Kinnikinnik. What a great name! It's just fun to say.

The dried leaves were used as a tobacco by the Ojibwa and at least 27 other tribes according to Daniel Moerman's amazing compendium, *Native American Ethnobotany*. He also cites references to the Cheyenne using the smoke to drive the evil spirits out of insane people, the Ojibwa smoking the roots to attract game and the Kwakiutl of the Pacific Northwest getting high on smoking the leaves.

p.s. Winter Ps

The evergreen leaves of Bearberry may allow some photosynthesis to occur during winter. We do know that blue-green light, which is ideal for chlorophyll absorption, penetrates snow to the greatest depth. Chlorophyll synthesis has been demonstrated to occur under as much as 32 inches of snow.

May	June	July

LAKE SUPERIOR'S SHORE
The Arctic Riviera

The Arctic was once in our own backyard. About 11,000 years ago, in the shadow of the glaciers, cold-adapted plants grew in profusion in Minnesota, Wisconsin and Michigan. As the great grinding glaciers moved north, the plants ranges flowed north with them. Most remnant populations in our area died off as the climate warmed. But there were survivors who found an arctic-like environment on the bare rocks of Lake Superior's North Shore and north-facing cliffs of the outer Apostle Islands. The year-round cold waters of Kitchi Gami create a micro-climate that mimics conditions far to the north around Hudson Bay.

The Splash Zone
Botanists refer to the remnant Lake Superior Ice Age flora as "Arctic relicts." They prefer the wave-splashed bare-rock shoreline where fog and chilled air sweeping across the cold lake keep summer temps ice-box cool. Lapping waves prevent trees and shrubs from gaining a foothold in the splash-zone, thereby keeping the niche open for our cold-adapted flora.

These penguins of the plant kingdom have special adaptations for cold comfort. Most are deep-rooted perennials that die back to ground level to prevent damage from winter ice. In the few days the temperature is over 43 degrees F—the minimum for photosynthesis—all of the Arctic relicts are able to flower, be fertilized and produce seeds. Some have evergreen leaves so that they do not have to waste energy on new growth. Others accumulate and store carbohydrates in underground corms. Amazing is the ability of some to track with the sun—focusing available heat on the reproductive flower parts—effectively giving them 25 percent more time for growth. Alpine Bistort (*Polygonum viviparum*) produces bulblets that are viable for reproduction, just in case the flowers are frozen out. Knotted Pearlwort (*Sagina nodosa*) can survive frozen roots.

Life on the Edge
Plant communities on cliffs can vary dramatically depending on if the rock is sedimentary limestone, metamorphic slate or igneous granite or basalt. The harsh environment is made even crueler by the lack of soil, exposure to wind and gravity. Most cliffs are either deep in the shade or baked by the sun. It takes a hardy plant to live life "on the edge."

Upland Goldenrod
Solidago ptarmicoides

Cheery clusters of these daisy-like goldenrods greet the lucky rock scrambler. Clumps of Upland Goldenrod look like escapees—fugitives from a nearby domestic flower garden. But don't be fooled, Upland Goldenrod is as wild as the rocky Lake Superior shores it inhabits.

June	July	August

Shrubby Cinquefoil
Potentilla fruticosa

This short shrub with sunny yellow flowers livens up many a North Shore point. It loves the cold and exposed rock ledges along Lake Superior.

Multipurpose Mouthwash

Native peoples treated weak bowels, bleeding, fevers and sore throats with Shrubby Cinquefoil. Evidently, some part of it was also used to make a mouthwash.

June	July	August

Even though it lives in a different habitat, has woody stems and different leaves, Shrubby Cinquefoil is still a close relative to Marsh Cinquefoil.

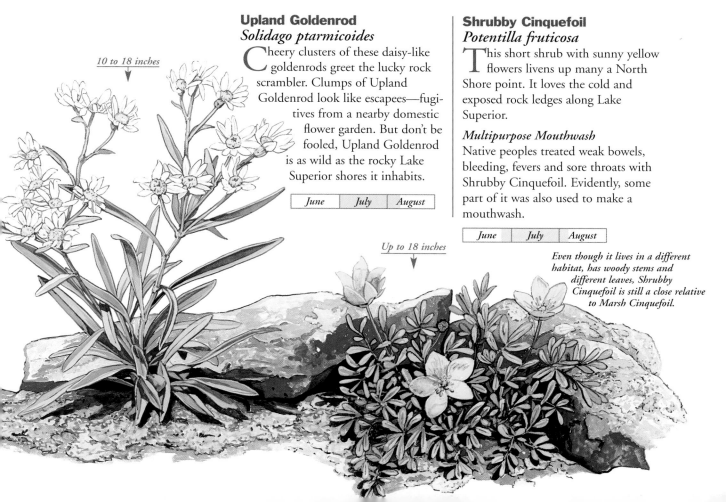

10 to 18 inches

Up to 18 inches

Three-toothed Cinquefoil
Potentilla tridentata

Our ground-hugging member of the Rose family grows in rock crevices in the North and at high elevations in the South. The leaves turn a vibrant red in autumn. Cooler temps found at elevation allow this little cinquefoil to survive on two mountaintops in extreme northern Georgia. "Old Three-tooth" is also at home in Greenland.

Note that the leaves have three tiny teeth at their tips.

Holy Comparison

Nicholas Culpeper, a 17th century physician, said of cinquefoil, "it is an herb of Jupiter, and therefore strengthens the parts of the body it rules: let a Jupiter be angular and strong when it is gather'd…, let no man despise it because it is plain and easy, the ways of God are all such."

June	July	August

A New Genus, Genius

Potentilla is a genus with over 500 species. Most are found in temperate or colder regions in the northern hemisphere. But some botanists believe this plant, with only three leaves, should not be grouped with the cinquefoils (five leaves) and suggest it be put in *Sibbaldia*, a related genus that shares Three-toothed Cinquefoil's characteristics of leaf type and style position.

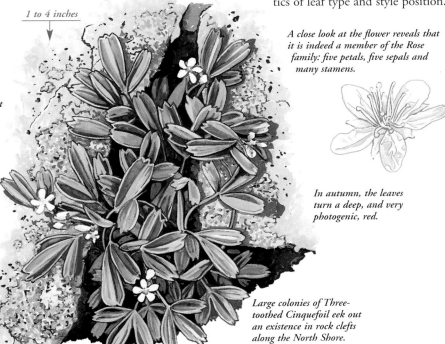

1 to 4 inches

A close look at the flower reveals that it is indeed a member of the Rose family: five petals, five sepals and many stamens.

In autumn, the leaves turn a deep, and very photogenic, red.

Large colonies of Three-toothed Cinquefoil eek out an existence in rock clefts along the North Shore.

Harebell
Campanula rotundifolia

It seems the steeper the cliff, the more Harebell is likely to call it home. Harebell is circumpolar; it grows from the Arrowhead of Minnesota east to the Appalachians, the fjords of Norway, all the way across Siberia to Asia and back to the Rocky Mountains.

In Scotland they call this cliff-dweller, the Bluebells-of-Scotland (surprise) and in Norway it is *blålokke*, which literally translates to "blue-bell." Other names include heathbells, heather-bells, lady's-thimble, round-leaved bellflower, wild-thimbles and witch's-bells.

The reference to round leaves (*rotundifolia*) may seem confusing at first since the leaves of an adult plant are very thin and grass-like. But the early leaves at the base of the plant are quite round.

6 to 12 inches

Origins of the name "hare-bell" are a little sketchier. It could be that hares like to frolic in the same barren habitat, or maybe it is referring to "hair-like" leaves, or could it be a derivation of the old Welsh name *awyr-pel* (balloon) or even a contraction of "heather bell" that ended up as "hea'erbell." I personally love the Ojibwa word for this plant, *ziginice*, which means "pouring."

Round basal leaves usually go unnoticed.

Harebells require only the tiniest dirt-filled crack to support themselves. They are true "rock hounds."

Unknowing Accomplices
Amazingly, big bumbling bumblebees are the main pollinators of the delicate Harebell. In their awkward attempts to access the down-facing flower, they must grab the long pistil to land, and, in the process, they are dusted with pollen from the stamens. At the next Harebell, the bee brushes up against the stigma, and becomes an unknowing accomplice in the task of cross pollination.

| June | July | August |

Butterwort
Pinguicula vulgaris

Tucked into crevices along rocky pools on Lake Superior's North Shore, Butterwort lives out its brief summer life in the very hostile environment of the "splash zone." But Butterwort has a few tricks up its "leaves." Sticky leaves help this carnivorous plant trap, dissolve and absorb soft insect tissue to get its recommended daily allowance of nitrogen and phosphorous. Purple flowers and yellowish basal leaves make this a very attractive plant...for a killer, that is.

Possibly named Butterwort for the feel of the slimy leaves, as if melted butter or fat was poured over them. The root of the genus *Pinguicula* is the Latin word for fat, *pinguis*.

2 to 5 inches

Udderly Ridiculous

In "ye olde times," Yorkshire farmers rubbed Butterwort juice on the udders of cows to encourage milk production. This folk remedy was also believed to protect cows from "elf arrows" and save humans from fairies and witches. Hmmm. I always thought fairies were good.

Sticky Situations

Butterwort's sticky, fleshy leaves trap tiny insects. The succulent leaves bear two types of glands: stalked glands that produce a sticky liquid that helps trap insects, and sessile glands that secrete enzymes needed to digest victims. Leaf edges curl over the "trapee" as the "trapper" secretes enzymes that extract nitrogen and other vital elements from the insect's body.

Phosphorous seems to be the most essential element the plant absorbs from the insect carcasses. Well-fed plants are also able to take up more nitrogen from the soil. Butterwort's leaves often die after trapping and digesting an insect. This may be because during the folded, "fake-stomach" period, the leaf is not photosynthesizing.

The flat, ground-hugging leaves of *Pinguicula* species are exceptionally good at capturing walking insects, especially *Acarina* (mites) and *Collembola* (springtails) species. Flying insects may be better adapted to escaping sticky situations.

Miniscule stalked glands on the leaves produce a sticky goo that traps insects. Other glands secrete enzymes used to digest the victims.

| June | July | August |

In a study by Antor and Garcia, Butterwort leaves were found to catch more prey than artificial sticky traps. The leaves must have an attractant. But what is this attractant? Is it the glistening sheen, an undetectable smell, the yellow leaves, an ultraviolet pattern or simply the fact that these insects prefer to forage on leaves rather than soil?

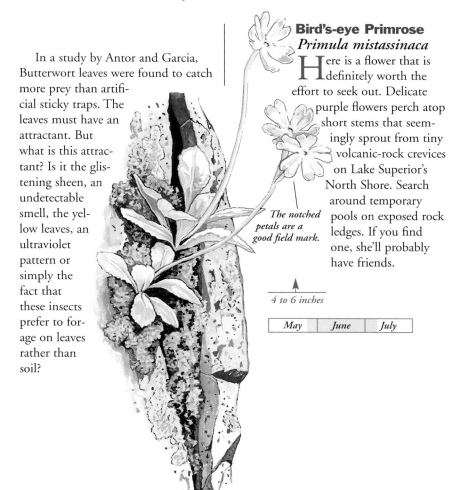

Bird's-eye Primrose
Primula mistassinaca

Here is a flower that is definitely worth the effort to seek out. Delicate purple flowers perch atop short stems that seemingly sprout from tiny volcanic-rock crevices on Lake Superior's North Shore. Search around temporary pools on exposed rock ledges. If you find one, she'll probably have friends.

The notched petals are a good field mark.

4 to 6 inches

| May | June | July |

Arctic Relicts
Gifts of the Glaciers

Both Bird's-eye Primrose and Butterwort are considered Arctic relicts because our Great Lakes populations are separated from their main ranges far to the North. Here are other northerners at home along the cold coasts of Lake Superior where postglacial conditions still exist.

Northern Anemone (Anemone parvilflora)
Heart-leaved Arnica (Arnica cordifolia)
Alpine Milk-Vetch (Astragalus alpinus)
Norwegian Whitlow Grass (Draba norvegica)
Yellow Mtn Avens (Dryas drummondii)
Smooth-lvd Mtn Avens (D. integrifolia)
Black Crowberry (Empetrum nigrum)
Purple Crowberry (E. autropurpureum)
Acrid Fleabane (Erigeron acris)
Hudson Bay Eyebright (Euphrasia hudsoniana)
Alpine Sweet-Vetch (Hedysarum alpinum)
Arctic Lupine (Lupinus arcticus)
Butterwort (Pinguicula vulgaris)
Alpine Bistort (Polygonum viviparum)
Bird's-eye Primrose (Primula mistassinica)
Arctic Wintergreen (Pyrola grandiflora)
Knotted Pearlwort (Sagina nodosa)
Prickly Saxifrage (Saxifraga tricuspidata)
Huron Tansy (Tanacetum huronense)
Common False Asphodel (Tofielda pusilla)

FIELDS & WAYSIDES
Roadside Warriors

Road salt, bulldozers, fire, mowing, pesticides and herbicides are just a few of the environmental hazards that our "roadside warriors" must deal with. No wonder European aliens dominate this habitat. (Look for the British flag next to immigrants.) Disturbed areas had been around for centuries in England where many of our aliens originated. North American plants had never known such a habitat. Though Great Britain is their home of origin, they are certainly bona-fide North American species now; so we might as well get used to it and learn to love them.

Ecosystems change and evolve. Birds such as Savannah Sparrows, Bobolinks and Eastern Meadowlarks, who were strictly tied to prairies in pre-Columbian times, have now adapted to hayfields and meadows that are dominated by European and Asian "weeds."

It is true that non-native plants often outcompete natives for resources, but should we take the attitude of Edwin Rollin Spencer, author of *All About Weeds*, when he states, "In the struggle for existence a bad weed is a prince. It has the traits of a Bonaparte or Hitler. Give it an inch and it will take a mile." Most aliens have found a niche in the waste areas of America. They are true "roadside warriors" and are here to stay.

One Man's Weed is another Man's Unloved Flower

No botanical division is reserved for "weeds." It is strictly a term of attitude. The weed quotes below put a positive spin on our less-loved plants.

"Flowers must not be too profuse nor obtrusive; else they acquire the reputation of weeds."
—Henry David Thoreau

"It is a plant out of place in the eye of man; in the nice eye of nature it is very much in place."
—Edwin Rollin Spencer

"A weed is no more than a flower in disguise."
—James Russell Lowell

"O thou weed! Who art so lovely fair and smell'st so sweet...[would] thou hadnst ne'er been born."
—William Shakespeare

"What is a weed? A plant whose virtues have not been discovered."
—Ralph Waldo Emerson

"A weed is but an unloved flower."
—Ella Wheeler Wilcox

Orange Hawkweed
Hieracium aurantiacum

King Devil
Hieracium piloselloides

Hawkweeds are members of the Compositae, but they have no tubular disk flowers, only flat ray flowers. King Devil and Orange Hawkweed are both aliens introduced to North America from Europe that have not only survived but THRIVED in waste areas and along roadsides.

Orange Hawkweed is commonly known as devil's-paintbrush and, less commonly, as artist's-brush, fairy's-paintbrush and venus'-paintbrush. I suppose all the paintbrush references come from the fact that unopened flower heads look like an artist's brush tipped with orange paint.

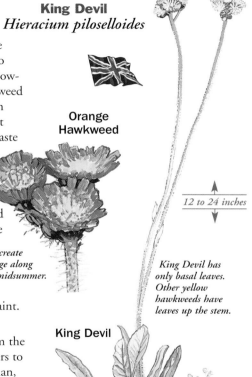

Orange Hawkweed

Dense stands create a sea of orange along roadways in midsummer.

12 to 24 inches

King Devil has only basal leaves. Other yellow hawkweeds have leaves up the stem.

King Devil

Hawkeye
The name "hawkweed" comes from the folk belief that hawks ate the flowers to improve their vision. Ancient Roman, Pliny the Elder, told of hawks tearing this plant apart and rubbing the juice on their eyes to clear their vision. In fact, the genus name *Hieracium* comes from the Greek *hierax* or "hawk."

Slimy Green Spacemen?
Orange Hawkweed is a toxin-exuding alien, and we're not talking about slimy green spacemen. The toxin helps limit competition among its neighbors and makes it unpalatable to grazers. This is a real advantage when growing in mass profusion where one needs to stake out turf. Farmers nicknamed Orange Hawkweed "devil's-paintbrush" due to their belief that it was an evil weed that even cows would not eat. Everything else was grazed down but the hawkweed was left standing tall.

May	June	July

June	July	August

Fireweed
Epilobium angustifolium

Only a few plants can bear flower buds, blossoms and seed pods on the same flower stalk at the same time. Fireweed flower buds open from the bottom of the stalk up, taking several weeks to reach the top. "When Fireweed blooms to the top, summer is over," the saying goes.

Any soil that has been disturbed, whether it is by bulldozer or wildfire, is a prime breeding ground for Fireweed. Fireweed's preference for disturbed sites such as railroad right-of-ways must have been the inspiration for the Swede's poetic name for it; *Rallarrøs,* which translates directly as "railroad-worker's rose." In rural America it has been known by many colorful names: Moose-tongue, blooming Sally, firetop, burntweed, purple-rocket, wickup and willow herb.

Mount St. Helens
Fireweed loves disturbance, and what could be more disturbing than when Mt. St. Helens erupted in 1980? The resulting ash-covered ground (the pyroclastic flow) was colonized early and heavily by Fireweed and Pearly Everlasting (*Anaphalis margaritacea*). Both species are pioneer plants whose seeds are wind-dispersed allowing them to travel great distances.

Trial by Fire
Wildfires leave behind a charred black landscape that may be ugly to some but is a perfect place for the wind-borne seeds of Fireweed. The sun-warmed soil is loaded with newly-released nutrients creating an ideal seedbed. Growth is explosive. Within weeks the black landscape is green, and by July, purple. Fireweed, Fringed Bindweed (*Polygonum cilinode*) and Large-leaved Aster not only beautify the burn but also stabilize bare soil that is vulnerable to severe erosion. But Fireweed does not need wildfire. It can grow on any disturbed site including roadsides, gravel pits and even urban ruins.

Fireweed blossom

36 to 72 inches

Seedpods, flowers and buds may all occupy space on a single spike.

London after WWII
A *New York Herald Tribune* article by Lewis Gannet from July 1944 gives an eyewitness account to the heart of bombed-out London:

"London, paradoxically, is the gayest where she has been the most blitzed. The wounds made this summer by flying bombs are, of course, still raw and bare, but cellars and courts shattered into

June	July	August

rubble by the German raids of 1940-'41 have been taken over by an army of [Fireweed plants] which have turned them into wild gardens, sometimes as gay as any tilled by human hands.... [Fireweed] sweeps across this pockmarked city and turns what might have been scars into flaming beauty."

Everything but the Kitchen Sink

Fireweed fluff (wind-dispersed feathery seeds) was mixed with mountain goat hair for weaving by some Canadian tribes. The Haida wove strips of the stem into twine and made fishing nets. Siberian Yakuts made a wicked ale from Fireweed and the poisonous/hallucinogenic Fly Amanita mushroom. They developed an entire cult around this potent concoction.

Young Fireweed shoots, when boiled or steamed, make an awesome asparagus-like vegetable. Add butter and salt and enjoy!

Wood Lily
Lilium philadelphicum

Trying to hide amongst the tall roadside grasses are the huge orange blossoms of the Wood Lily. The name Wood Lily is a bit of a misnomer as they are rare in the shadowed haunts of the forest, preferring sunny locations. A few of these other names seem more appropriate: fire lily, flame lily, freckled lily, glade lily, orange-cup lily, tiger lily and prairie lily.

All Bark and No Bite... Anymore

"Hmmm, how can I get back at that dog that just bit me?" I can hear the poor Ojibwa victim lament. Well, according to early twentieth-century researcher Melvin

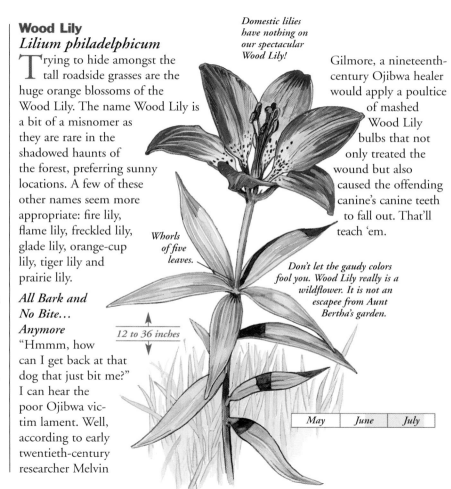

Domestic lilies have nothing on our spectacular Wood Lily!

Whorls of five leaves.

12 to 36 inches

Don't let the gaudy colors fool you. Wood Lily really is a wildflower. It is not an escapee from Aunt Bertha's garden.

| May | June | July |

Gilmore, a nineteenth-century Ojibwa healer would apply a poultice of mashed Wood Lily bulbs that not only treated the wound but also caused the offending canine's canine teeth to fall out. That'll teach 'em.

Common Evening-Primrose
Oenothera biennis

Flower parts in fours is an important clue to placing Common Evening-Primrose in the family Onagraceae; members have four petals, four sepals, four (or eight) stamens and a four-parted stigma. Surprisingly, it is not a member of the Primrose family.

Interesting folk names include evening-star, king's cure-all, four-o-clock, golden-candlestick and night willow-herb. I especially like the name the Swedes give it—*nattjus* or "night light."

The Sphinx Comes a' Callin'

Taking the opposite tack of most flowers, evening-primroses open fully at dusk inviting nocturnal sphinx moths (family Sphingidae), to come in, feed and perform their pollination magic.

Of course, all the sphinx moth wants is a sip of yummy nectar. Conveniently, the sweet treat is at the bottom of the corolla and the moth has to stick its head in close. The proboscis becomes dusted with pollen which is brushed off on the stigma of the next flower visited, thereby accomplishing cross-fertilization. Flowers are so tricky.

Dusk is when the flowers open completely. This allows access to the hummingbird-like sphinx moths.

36 to 60 inches

| June | July | August |

Wild Lupine
Lupinus polyphyllus

Lupinus polyphyllus is a native species of the western states that has been widely cultivated in the East. It easily escapes and can line roadsides in a dizzying array of pinks, purples and blues. Large patches become celebrities.

18 to 30 inches

Lupine flowers can be pink, blue or purple.

Vernacular names include Quaker-bonnets, monkey-faces, wild pea and old-maid's-bonnets.

Praise from the Ancients

Ancient Egyptians cultivated lupines as a food source. Pliny, the Roman senator, historian, naval commander and naturalist, claimed that no food was more wholesome or easier to digest, and that they produced a 'fresh' complexion and a cheerful countenance.

Okay. Totally unrelated, but did you know that Pliny the Elder died from poisonous gasses as his ship was attempting to rescue the citizens of Pompeii when Mt. Vesuvius erupted in 79 AD? He left the world with over 160 volumes of observations on history and nature. My kind of guy.

May	June	July

Bird's-foot Trefoil
Lotus corniculatus

Our lemon yellow legume of the Bean (or Pea) family enjoys company; it can be found growing in great profusion along the edges of paved and unpaved roads alike.

You can really see Bird's-foot Trefoil's Bean family heritage in its flowers and leaves.

Crow Toes and Devil's Fingers

Its odd name comes from the bunches of hooked bean pods that reminded some of the claws of a bird's foot. Avian toes are not the only object people believed the seedpod or flower resembled; other names include bird's-eye, cross-toes, crow-toes, devil's-fingers, ladies-fingers, sheep-foot and shoes-and-stockings. Many of the above names originated in the British Isles, its native home. *Lotus corniculatus* is known by over 70 common names in England.

June	July	August

6 to 12 inches

Brown-eyed Susan
Rudbeckia hirta

Originally a wildflower of the prairie, this sun-lover moved east with the clearing of the great forests. Today it is found from Newfoundland to Florida and west to British Columbia. It is the state flower of Maryland. She is also known as brown Betty and black-eyed Susan.

Brown-eyed Susan's True Identity Revealed...Olav Rudbeck!

Linnaeus first described Brown-eyed Susan in his landmark 1753 work, *Species Plantarum*. He named the genus *Rudbeckia* after two professors who preceded him at the University of Uppsala, Sweden: Olav Rudbeck and his son.

July	August	Sept

This is not just one flower. Dozens of brown "disk flowers" form the center while yellow petaled "ray flowers" ring the outside edge.

12 to 30 inches

Ox-eye Daisy
Leucanthemum vulgare

Some consider it a weed, others, a roadside beauty, but botanically speaking Ox-eye Daisy is a non-native member of the Composite family that was introduced to North American from Europe. In fact, it may be one of the earliest European escapees on our continent. In August of 1631, John Winthrop Jr., the son of the first governor of Massachusetts Bay Colony, bought a bunch of flower and vegetable seeds from a London merchant. Three months later he landed in New England with the seeds. Included on the bill of sale were "basil, cabedg, lettice, radish, spynadg, cullumbine, hollyhocks, marigold and a half ounce of maudlin [Ox-eye Daisy] seeds." The seeds were planted in North American soil in the spring of 1632 and the first "wild" Ox-eye Daisy probably soon followed.

The name "daisy" comes from "ye olde English." Chaucer wrote of the "dayes eye" or "eye of day" when referring to the flowers of this family. The English translation of its former Latin name (*Chrysanthemum leucanthemum*) was literally "gold-flowered white flower." But today it is no longer considered a chrysanthemum; Ox-eye Daisy is now known as *Leucanthemum vulgare.*

Other common names for our bright-eyed alien are butter daisy, field daisy and moon daisy

English naturalist Marcus Woodward wrote "the flower, with its white rays and golden disc, has small resemblance to an ox's eye, but at dusk it shines out from the mowing-grass like a fallen moon." Nineteenth-century poets referred to the "snows of June" in reference to the blizzard of white Ox-eye Daisies covering the fields.

Gool Riders
Ox-eye Daisies were much hated by the

*Ambush! Goldenrod Crab Spiders (*Misumena vatia*), who can change their own body color to match either yellow or white flowers, often use Ox-eye Daisies as a perch for ambushing unwary bees and flies. Closely examine a patch in late summer and you will likely encounter a hunting crab spider.*

Scottish farmers who called the plants "gools" and hired gool-riders to enforce daisy-removal laws. The farmer with the biggest crop of gools was fined one castrated ram. But the daisies were appreciated in Europe for one reason: bunches of Ox-eye Daisy were hung inside houses and barns to keep away lightning.

He Loves Me...He Loves Me Not
The children's fortune-telling game "He loves me, He loves me not" most likely originated with the common daisy. The last petal plucked foretold their loves true desire. But this was not the only role of the daisy. A text from 1696 instructs lonelyhearts to place "dazy roots under their pillow" in order to have pleasant dreams of loved ones.

Mary Magdalen's Daisy
The ancients dedicated this plant to the goddess of women, Artemis, because it is useful in treating "women's complaints." With the rise of Christianity it was rededicated to honor St. Mary Magdalen, the repentant prostitute and witness to Christ's resurrection. It was known as Maudlin daisy or Maudlinwort.

Green sheathing-bracts protect the flower from insects who would chew their way to the nectar from below rather than from above and thereby pollinating the plant.

12 to 24 inches

| June | July | August |

White Sweet Clover & Yellow Sweet Clover
Melilotus alba (White) & Melilotus officinalis (Yellow)

Yellow Sweet Clover was first recorded in North America in 1664! The early colonists imported the plants from Europe (White Sweet Clover) and the Mediterranean region (Yellow Sweet Clover) as forage crops for livestock. Since the 1800s the plants have been widely grown as a crop and soil builder. They have spread widely and today carpet fields and open roadsides throughout our area. Sweet clovers can also be found in Australia and temperate parts of Asia. It is a preferred honeybee forage plant.

Others have called them honey plants, honey clover, king's-crown and king's clover.

Sweet and Sinister
Roll down your window as you drive a clover-lined road and you will smell the reason these twins are called sweet clovers. The odor can be quite powerful and is due to a chemical called coumarin, which also gives the pleasant odor to sweet grass (*Hierochloe* species), bedstraws (*Galium* species) and fresh cut hay.

But this pleasure-giving chemical can turn deadly if the cut clover is allowed to rot. Coumarin breaks down into compounds that prevent blood clotting. Livestock feeding on hay comprised of rotting clover can bleed to death from even a minor injury. The biochemical explanation is that molds such as certain penicilliums metabolize coumarin into dicoumarin, which prevents vitamin K formation. Vitamin K is absolutely necessary to activate prothrombin, which aids in clotting blood.

Research on this phenomenon led to the discovery of the drug dicoumarol and its eventual use as an important anti-clotting agent.

Coumarin is also a main ingredient in rat poison and was even added to cigarette tobacco at one time. Abraham Lincoln's mother is rumored to have died by drinking tainted milk from a cow that had eaten rotten sweet clover.

White Sweet Clover

Yellow Sweet Clover

Sweet clovers scent the scenic summer highways and byways.

Sweet clovers are a popular hay crop...but beware; rotting sweet clover hay can be deadly to cattle.

24 to 96 inches

| June | July | August |

Butter & Eggs
Linaria vulgaris

Butter & Eggs is found in places where you'd never find real butter or real eggs. It is common along roadways, vacant lots and alleys—even growing up through the asphalt on occasion.

If the shape of the flowers looks familiar, it may be because they are in the same family as your domestic, garden snapdragon. The two-toned yellow and white flowers are probably the inspiration behind the wonderfully goofy name of Butter & Eggs. Others have put a spin on this theme with the names bread-and-butter and eggs-and-bacon. Less gastronomically-inspired names include dead-man's-bones (Scotland), hogmouth, rabbit-ears, wax-candles and yellow toadflax. Thank goodness for Latin names!

Aggressive Alien

In a short 1758 paper with a not-so-brief title—*A brief account of those plants that are most troublesome in our pastures and fields, in Pennsylvania; most of which were brought from Europe*—John

Bartram writes about the European invaders, "the most mischievous of these is, first, the stinking yellow *Linaria*. It is the most hurtful plant to our pastures that can grow in our northern climate. Neither the spade, plough, nor hoe can eradicate it when it is spread in pasture. Every little fiber that is left will soon increase prodigiously." Since then it has spread quickly across southern Canada and the entire United States.

June	July	August

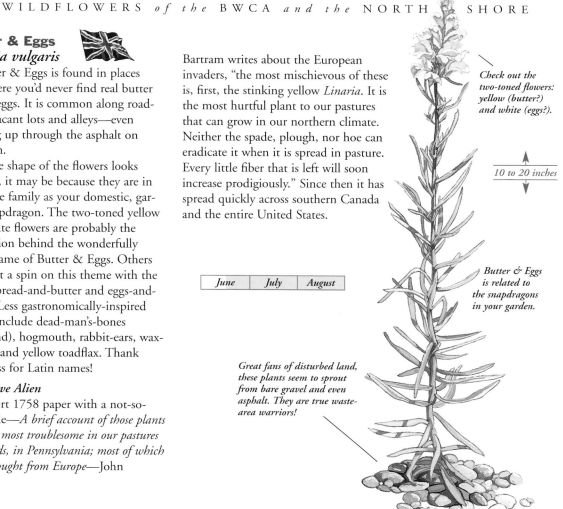

Check out the two-toned flowers: yellow (butter?) and white (eggs?).

10 to 20 inches

Butter & Eggs is related to the snapdragons in your garden.

Great fans of disturbed land, these plants seem to sprout from bare gravel and even asphalt. They are true waste-area warriors!

Tansy
Tanacetum vulgare

Dense stands of Tansy may be found in sunny waste areas throughout the North Woods. The numerous yellow flower heads dry to pungent brown buttons in fall. Crush one in your hand and inhale the scent deeply.

Local names in England include gold-buttons, hindheal, parsley-fern ginger plant and bitter-buttons.

Easter Cakes
An English author writing in 1931 told of an old and unique Easter-season tradition. After Lent, handball games would be played between men of the congregation; sometimes even bishops and archbishops would join in. The victor would win Tansy cakes, a mixture of the young leaves and eggs, which were said to "purify the humours" after the Spartan diet of Lent.

More Lore of Yore.
Civil War lore contends that dried Tansy heads were crushed up and sprinkled in the tracks of horses carrying the dead to mask the pungent odor. I can't vouch for how effective that technique may have been, but Tansy leaves do

contain an effective natural insect repellent. Manasseh Cutler wrote in 1785, "fresh meat may be preserved from the attacks of the flesh-fly, by rubbing it with this plant."

Powerful Stuff
Ojibwa hunters smoked a concoction that included Tansy flowers to attract deer. The Ojibwa medicine man also used the roots to make drops for sore ears, an infusion of the leaves to break a fever, and a decoction of leaves to stop menstruation. The dried root was chewed for sore throats.

For a real "scent sensation" crush some flower heads and inhale..

24 to 48 inches

July	August	Sept

Common Yarrow
Achillea millefolium

It is widely believed that Yarrow came to North America from Europe with the early colonists. Today, it can be found in nearly every disturbed area that gets a bit of sun. We may despise this plant because of its abundance, but once you read about this common "weed's" amazing traits of you may have a new appreciation of the lowly Yarrow.

"A thousand leaves" is the literal translation of Yarrow's specific name, *millefolium*, and refers to the finely divided, lacey leaves.

All Hail "The Coagulator!"
Yarrow contains an amazing chemical called achilleine that speeds the formation of blood clots—a trait that has given rise to common names such as bloodwort, soldier's-woundwort (used during the American Civil War to stop bleeding), nosebleed plant and carpen-

ter's weed (to clot blood of careless woodworkers). Interestingly, the old Gaelic name for Yarrow, *lus chosgadh na fola,* means "plant that stops bleeding."

Achille's Heal
(Get it?…Heal…not Heel)

Yarrow made Achilles. The Greek hero has been credited with discovering the plant's blood-clotting ability outside the Walls of Troy. But others say it was the centaur physician Chiron who clued Achilles in to Yarrow's miraculous benefits. When he and his men attacked Troy in 1200 B.C. to free Helen of Greece (Helen of Troy), Achilles used Yarrow to heal his warriors. It may be that his knowledge and use of this healing herb during the Trojan War elevated him to legend status. Too bad his heels were so vulnerable.

Fever Breaker

In northern Europe, depression and melancholy are treated with Yarrow tea. One of the best herbal fever-breakers there is, Yarrow tea contains the alkaloid, achilleine, which promotes perspiration. Herbalists also tout it as an excellent uterine toner.

12 to 36 inches

Millefolium means "thousand leaves." The finely divided individual leaves do give one that impression.

Stimulating in Life and Death

Domestic varieties of Yarrow (pink, red, etc.) when planted in gardens seem to stimulate the growth of neighboring plants and make herbs taste better. On the other side of the garden fence, Yarrow leaves mixed with compost significantly speed up decomposition .

Crystal Ball of the Plant World

This sometimes-despised weed of vacant lots has a long history of revered use in the world. Fortune telling was one trait ascribed to Yarrow.

The Druids believed it could foretell upcoming weather. The ancient Chinese book of prophecy, *I Ching*, claimed it could be used to predict the future. The stems were tossed and the resulting pattern interpreted. A ritual performed by Scottish Highland girls was said to allow them to dream of their true love. The Yarrow was "cut with a black-handled knife, by moonlight, repeating mystic words. It was then brought home, put into the right stocking, and placed under the pillow."

Herb-gathering Starlings

Recent research has shown that male European Starlings in North America go out of their way to gather Yarrow, certain goldenrods (*Solidago*

July	August	Sept

species) and fleabane (*Erigeron* species). They place the fresh greenery in their nests. What is the advantage of this behavior?

Researchers found that these plants, when placed in plastic bags with nest material, delayed mite larvae emergence. Other strong-smelling plants did not.

The Starling-preferred greenery all contained volatile oils that are known to be bad news for mites, lice and bacteria such as streptococcus and staphylococcus. Starlings are evidently able to detect the oils with their well-developed (for a bird) sense of smell.

A German study through the Max-Planck Society's Research Unit for Ornithology found that aromatic herbs, like Yarrow, seem to boost a nestling's immune system and increase levels of red blood cells and basophil blood cells that help birds survive malnutrition and extreme weather.

Common Mullein
Verbascum thapsus

Biennial giant, Common Mullein takes two growing seasons to fully mature. A rosette of fuzzy basal leaves forms during the first season. But watch out. The following summer the mullein stalk shoots up four to seven feet.

The accepted common name is Common Mullein and is believed to have originated with the Latin name for leprosy—*mulandrum*—a disease which mullein was thought to cure.

The names flannel-leaf, velvet-leaf, Adam's-flannel and old-man's-flannel are obviously inspired by the furry, soft basal leaves, while Jacob's-staff, torches and candlewicks were in reference to the taller-than-a-man stalks.

Mullein blossoms

July	August	Sept

Sword Fight!
Asthma patients of yore inhaled the smoke of dried mullein leaves to ease symptoms.

And on a lighter note...who hasn't used the dried flower stalks as sabres in a mock sword fight with your buddy?

36 to 84 inches

Sparky's Quick and Simple Goldenrod Key

Goldenrods *Solidago* species

Naturalist, scientist and educator, Edwin Rollin Spencer made a profound and oh-so-true statement about the family of goldenrods in his book *All About Weeds*, "He is blind indeed who does not know goldenrod, but he is a taxonomist if he knows ALL the goldenrods." At least ten species call the North Woods home with over 90 species in North America. Most bloom late in the summer and linger into fall. Some are still holding their own come October.

Solidago is from the Latin *solidare* meaning "to join or make solid" and is in reference to an obscur medicinal use.

Goldenrods growing in the woods (e.g. Zigzag Goldenrod) commit far less of their tissue to flower production (eight to 20 percent) than old-field species (up to 30 percent).

Feather-veined Leaves

A. Leaflets in axils of leaves.

  B. Plume-like flower cluster. Narrow, untoothed upper leaves. Stem and leaves smooth. Roadsides. One and a half to 4 feet tall. **Early Goldenrod** (*Solidago juncea*)

  B. Wand-like flower cluster. Stem densely covered with hairs. Rough gray-green leaves. Dry soil. One to 2 feet tall. **Gray Goldenrod** (*Solidago nemoralis*)

A. Flower stalks in axils of leaves.

  C. Smooth stalk. Zigzag stem. Broad leaves. Understory of woodlands. One to 3 feet tall. **Zigzag Goldenrod** (*Solidago flexicaulis*)

  C. Hairy stem & leaves. Rocky slopes. One to 3 feet tall. **Hairy Goldenrod** (*Solidago hispida*)

Parallel-veined Leaves

A. Plume-like flower cluster.

  B. Leaves sparse and finely-toothed. Stem purplish or pale green and smooth. Moist ground. Two to 7 feet tall. **Late Goldenrod** (*Solidago gigantea*)

  B. Leaves dense and deeply-toothed. Stem smooth at base and downy up higher. Roadsides and meadows. One to 5 feet tall. **Canada Goldenrod** (*Solidago canadensis*)

Sparky's Quick and Simple Aster Key

Asters *Aster* species

"Asterisk," "asteroid" and "astronaut" are all words that have their etymological roots in the Greek word for star: *aster*. The radiating blue or white ray flowers must have reminded someone of the stars in the heavens.

There are over 150 species of asters in the United States and 600 species worldwide.

The Economy of Flowers

Woodland asters have far fewer flower heads than their old-field cousins. Why is this? Asters, such as Large-leaved Aster, live in a stable forest environment where it pays to invest most of your energy in large leaves and deep roots—traits that lead to a long life. In other words, woodland asters can afford to spend less energy on flower heads when they have a longer time frame to pass on their genes. This is the "stable-habitat" strategy.

But in areas such as roadsides and pastures that could be obliterated tomorrow, it is better to "make hay while the sun shines," as one author put it, and produce as many seed heads as possible, leading to better chances of survival. This is the "opportunistic" strategy.

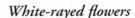

Blue or purple-rayed flowers

A. Lower leaves have a petiole and are heart-shaped or truncated;

  B. Lower leaves with pronounced winged-petiole. Stem purple. Flower heads clustered at top. Dry soils. Two to 4 feet tall.
Fringed Blue Aster *(Aster ciliolatus)*

  B. Upper leaves sessile and broadly oval. Lower leaves very large and broad with rough undersides. Two to 4 feet.
Large-leaved Aster *(Aster macrophyllus)*

A. Lower leaves clasping stem and sessile;

  B. Leaves toothed and rough. Stem usually purple and bristly. Swamps and wet thickets. Two to 7 feet tall.
Purple-stemmed Aster *(Aster puniceus)*

White-rayed flowers

A. Flowers in a flat cluster at top;

  B. Leaves lance-shaped, duller green with a textured surface and rough edge. Flowers have few rays (2 to 15). Disks yellow, sometimes turning purplish. Two to 7 feet.
Flat-topped White Aster *(Aster umbellatus)*

A. Flowers in panicles (side stems off main stem);

  C. Leaves thin—willow-like—and mostly untoothed;

    D. Rays long and numerous (20 to 40). Flower large (3/4-inch) with yellow disks. Damp ground. Three to 8 feet.
Panicled Aster *(Aster lanceolatus)*

  C. Leaves toothed and wider;

    E. Rays short and numerous. Flower small (to 3/8-inch) with deep purple disks. Many flower heads. One to 3 feet.
Calico Aster *(Aster lateriflorus)*

Flower Types & Parts

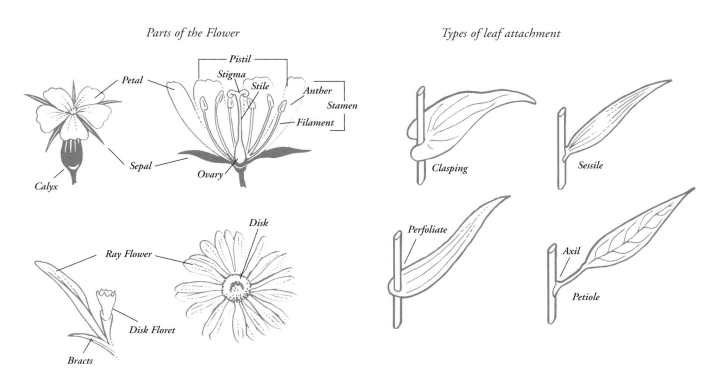

Parts of the Flower

Petal

Pistil

Stigma

Stile

Anther

Stamen

Filament

Sepal

Calyx

Ovary

Ray Flower

Disk

Disk Floret

Bracts

Types of leaf attachment

Clasping

Sessile

Perfoliate

Axil

Petiole

Checklist of North Woods Flora

Alismataceae—Water-plantain Family
- o Broad-leaved Arrowhead (*Sagittaria latifolia*)

Araceae—Arum Family
- o Jack-in-the-Pulpit (*Arisaema triphyllum*)
- o Wild Calla (*Calla palustris*)
- o Skunk Cabbage (*Symplocarpus foetidus*)

Araliaceae—Ginseng Family
- o Bristly Sarsaparilla (*Aralia hispida*)
- o Wild Sarsaparilla (*Aralia nudicaulis*)
- o Dwarf Ginseng (*Panax trifolium*)

Aristolochiaceae—Birthwort Family
- o Wild Ginger (*Asarum canadense*)

Asclepiadaceae—Milkweed Family
- o Swamp Milkweed (*Asclepias incarnata*)

Balsaminaceae—Touch-me-not Family
- o Spotted Touch-me-not (*Impatiens capensis*)

Betulaceae—Birch Family
- o Bog Birch (*Betula glandulifera*)

Campanulaceae—Bluebell Family
- o Harebell (*Campanula rotundifolia*)

Caprifoliaceae—Honeysuckle Family
- o Twinflower (*Linnaea borealis*)

Compositae—Composite or Daisy Family
- o Common Yarrow (*Achillea millefolium*)
- o Large-leaved Aster (*Aster macrophyllus*)
- o Asters (*Aster* species)
- o Spotted Joe-Pye Weed (*Eupatorium maculatum*)
- o Orange Hawkweed (*Hieracium aurantiacum*)
- o King Devil (*Hieracium piloselloides*)
- o Ox-eye Daisy (*Leucanthemum vulgare*)
- o Brown-eyed Susan (*Rudbeckia hirta*)
- o Upland Goldenrod (*Solidago ptarmicoides*)
- o Goldenrods (*Solidago* species)
- o Tansy (*Tanacetum vulgare*)

Cornaceae—Dogwood Family
- o Bunchberry (*Cornus canadensis*)

Cyperaceae—Sedge Family
- o Cotton-Grasses (*Eriophorum* species)

Droseraceae—Sundew Family
- o Round-leaved Sundew (*Drosera rotundifolia*)

Ericaceae—Heath Family
- o Bog Rosemary (*Andromeda glaucophylla*)
- o Bearberry (*Arctostaphylos uva-ursi*)
- o Leatherleaf (*Chamaedaphne calyculata*)
- o Wintergreen (*Gaultheria procumbens*)
- o Bog Laurel (*Kalmia polifolia*)
- o Labrador Tea (*Ledum groenlandicum*)
- o Velvet-leaved Blueberry (*Vaccinium myrtilloides*)
- o Small-fruited Bog Cranberry (*Vaccinium oxycoccus*)

Fumariaceae—Fumitory Family
- o Pale Corydalis (*Corydalis sempervirens*)
- o Dutchman's Breeches (*Dicentra cucullaria*)

Hypericaceae—St. Johnswort Family
- o Marsh St. Johnswort (*Triadenum virginicum*)

Iridaceae—Iris Family
- o Wild Iris (*Iris versicolor*)

Labiatae—Mint Family
- o Marsh Skullcap (*Scutellaria galericulata*)

Leguminosae—Bean or Pea Family
- o Bird's-foot Trefoil (*Lotus corniculatus*)
- o Wild Lupine (*Lupinus polyphyllus*)
- o White Sweet Clover (*Melilotus alba*)
- o Yellow Sweet Clover (*Melilotus officinalis*)

Lentibulariaceae—Bladderwort Family
- o Butterwort (*Pinguicula vulgaris*)
- o Greater Bladderwort (*Utricularia vulgaris*)

Liliaceae—Lily Family
- o Wild Leek (*Allium tricoccum*)
- o Clintonia (*Clintonia borealis*)
- o White Trout Lily (*Erythronium albidum*)
- o Yellow Trout Lily (*Erythronium americanum*)
- o Wood Lily (*Lilium philadelphicum*)
- o Canada Mayflower (*Maianthemum canadense*)
- o Bog Solomon's-Seal (*Smilacina trifolia*)
- o Rose Twisted-Stalk (*Streptopus roseus*)
- o Large-flowered Trillium (*Trillium grandiflorum*)
- o Large-flowered Bellwort (*Uvularia perfoliata*)
- o Sessile Bellwort (*Uvularia sessilifolia*)

Menyanthaceae—Buckbean Family
- o Buckbean or Bogbean (*Menyanthes trifoliata*)

Nymphaeaceae—Water-Lily Family
- o Water Shield (*Brasenia schreberi*)
- o Fragrant White Water-Lily (*Nymphaea odorata*)
- o Common White Water-Lily (*Nymphaea tuberosa*)
- o Bullhead Lily (*Nuphar luteum* or *N. variegatum*)

Onagraceae—Evening-primrose Family
- o Fireweed (*Epilobium angustifolium*)
- o Common Evening-Primrose (*Oenothera biennis*)

Orchidaceae—Orchid Family
- o Arethusa (*Arethusa bulbosa*)
- o Grass-Pink or Swamp-Pink (*Calopogon tuberosus*)
- o Calypso (*Calypso bulbosa*)
- o Spotted Coralroot (*Corallorhiza maculata*)
- o Pink Ladyslipper (*Cypripedium acaule*)
- o Rose Pogonia (*Pogonia ophioglossoides*)

Papaveraceae—Poppy Family
- o Bloodroot (*Sanguinaria canadensis*)

Polygonaceae—Buckwheat Family
- o Water Smartweed (*Polygonum amphibium*)

Pontederiaceae—Pickerelweed Family
- o Pickerelweed (*Pontederia cordata*)

Portulacaceae—Purslane Family
- o Carolina Spring Beauty (*Claytonia caroliniana*)
- o Spring Beauty (*Claytonia virginica*)

Checklist of North Woods Flora

Primulaceae—Primrose Family
- o Fringed Loosestrife (*Lysimachia ciliata*)
- o Swamp Candles (*Lysimachia terrestris*)
- o Tufted Loosestrife (*Lysimachia thyrsiflora*)
- o Bird's-eye Primrose (*Primula mistassinaca*)
- o Starflower (*Trientalis borealis*)

Pyrolaceae—Wintergreen Family
- o Pipsissewa (*Chimaphila umbellate*)
- o One-flowered Wintergreen (*Moneses uniflora*)
- o Indian Pipe (*Monotropa uniflora*)
- o Pink Pyrola (*Pyrola asarifolia*)
- o Shinleaf (*Pyrola elliptica*)

Ranunculaceae—Buttercup Family
- o Red Baneberry (*Actaea rubra*)
- o Wood Anemone (*Anemone quinquefolia*)
- o Wild Columbine (*Aquilegia canadensis*)
- o Marsh Marigold (*Caltha palustris*)
- o Round-lobed Hepatica (*Hepatica americana*)

Rosaceae—Rose Family
- o Wood Strawberry (*Fragaria vesca*)
- o Meadow Strawberry (*Fragaria virginiana*)
- o Shrubby Cinquefoil (*Potentilla fruticosa*)
- o Marsh Cinquefoil (*Potentilla palustris*)
- o Three-toothed Cinquefoil (*Potentilla tridentata*)
- o American Red Raspberry (*Rubus idaeus*)
- o Thimbleberry (*Rubus parviflorus*)
- o Dewberry or Dwarf Raspberry (*Rubus pubescens*)

Sarraceniaceae—Pitcher-Plant Family
- o Pitcher Plant (*Sarracenia purpurea*)

Saxifragaceae—Saxifrage Family
- o Richardson's Alumroot (*Heuchera richardsonii*)
- o Skunk Currant (*Ribes glandulosum*)

Scheuchzeriaceae—Podgrass Family
- o Bog Scheuchzeria (*Scheuchzeria palustris*)

Scrophulariaceae—Figwort Family
- o Butter & Eggs (*Linaria vulgaris*)
- o Common Mullein (*Verbascum thapsus*)

Umbelliferae—Carrot or Parsley Family
- o Water Hemlock (*Cicuta maculata*)

Violaceae—Violet Family
- o Early Sweet White Violet (*Viola macloskeyi*)
- o Downy Yellow Violet (*Viola pubescens*)
- o Wooly Blue Violet (*Viola sororia*)

Titles of Interest

Chadde, Steve W. 1998. *A Great Lakes Wetland Flora*. Calumet, MI: Pocketflora Press.

> A 569-page comprehensive guide to our wet and wild areas. Kudos to Steve for including grasses, sedges and ferns, All pen-and-ink illustrations; no photos.

Morley, Thomas. 1966 (1969). *Spring Flora of Minnesota*. Minneapolis, MN: University of Minnesota Press.

> No photos or illustrations, but fantastic simplified keys to all our spring flora including grasses.

Newmaster, Steven G., Allen G. Harris and Linda J. Kershaw. 1997. *Wetland Plants of Ontario*. Edmonton, AB: Lone Pine Publishing.

> Photos, illustrations and natural history notes, all in a field-guide-sized book. And don't let the title fool you; Ontario's flora is basically the same as ours.

Oslund, Clayton and Michele Oslund. 2001. *What's Doin' the Bloomin'? A Pictorial Guide to Wildflowers of the Upper Great Lakes*. Duluth, Minnesota: Plant Pics.

> A wonderful home reference (a little too big for day hikes) with photos actually large enough to be useful!

Ownby, G.B. and T. Morley. 1991. *Vascular Plants of Minnesota: A Checklist and Atlas*. Minneapolis, MN: University of Minnesota Press.

> The "bible" of Minnesota plant distribution. A map for every species and a dot for every collection site.

Peterson, Roger Tory and Margaret McKenny. 1968. *A Field Guide to Wildflowers of Northeastern and North-central North America*. Boston, MA: Houghton-Mifflin Company.

> My favorite. It goes in my backpack on every day hike.

Shubat, Deborah and Gary Walton. 1997. *Rare Plants of Minnesota's Arrowhead*. Duluth, MN: Olga Lakela Herbarium, University of Minnesota-Duluth.

> A tiny spiral bound book that is out of print. The 56 very rare species are illustrated with color photocopies of pressed herbarium specimens. Maps show collection sites.

Smith, Welby R. 1993. *Orchids of Minnesota*. Minneapolis, MN: University of Minnesota Press.

> A must-have for the orchid enthusiast. Detailed species accounts. Beautiful photos of many, but not all, species.

Stensaas, Mark Sparky. 1996. *Canoe Country Flora: Plants and Trees of the North Woods and Boundary Waters*. Minneapolis, MN: University of Minnesota Press.

> More natural history about the trees, shrubs, flowers, moss, ferns, lichens and fungi of the North.

Walshe, Shan. 1980. *Plants of Quetico and the Ontario Shield*. Toronto, ON: University of Toronto Press.

> Now in paperback. This is a classic by the late great Canadian naturalist, Shan Walshe. Many photos arranged in habitats. Notes on the plant's preferred soil type.

Glossary

alien: Plant that was introduced to North America from another part of the world.

anther: Widened tip of the stamen that holds the pollen.

axil: The point where leaf and stem connect.

basal rosette: Ring of ground-hugging leaves at the base of the stem.

bracts: Modified leaves adjacent to the flower. Often green.

catkin: A hanging cluster of tiny male flowers on shrubs and trees.

corm: A bulbous, underground stem-growth that stores nutrients for future roots, leaves and flowers. Common in spring ephemerals.

cotyledon: A seed leaf, which stores or absorbs food for a growing plant.

disk flower: Tiny flowers that are found en masse in the center of members of the Composite family (e.g. daisies).

drupelets: Fleshy, round part of a fruit found clustered together as in raspberries and dewberries.

genus: The first name in a plant's scientific name. Taxonomic group between family and species.

inflorescence: Entire cluster of flowers on a single plant.

petiole: Stem of a leaf.

pistil: Female organ of a flower. Comprised of a stigma, style and ovary.

pollinium: Sticky, pollen-bearing package found in orchids.

ray flower: Tiny flowers with large, showy outer petals that ring the flower head of members of the Composite family (e.g. daisies).

sepal: Small petal-like leaf that is below the petals. Usually green. Sometimes showy and large as in Bunchberry.

sessile: Leaf attaches directly to plant stem. The leaf has no petiole.

spadix: Club-shaped spike covered with tiny flowers. Only in the members of the Arum family (e.g. Jack-in-the-Pulpit, Wild Calla and Skunk Cabbage).

spathe: Hood-like sheath that shields the spadix. Only in the members of the Arum family (e.g. Jack-in-the-Pulpit, Wild Calla and Skunk Cabbage).

specific epithet: Second Latin name in a flower's scientific name.

stamen: Male organ of a flower. Comprised of a filament and a pollen-bearing anther.

stigma: Tip of the female pistil that receives the pollen.

stomata: Tiny openings in leaves that allow for gas and water exchange.

symbiosis: Two plants living together in a mutually beneficial relationship (e.g. lichens are composed of a fungus and and algae).

tuber: A fleshy enlarged portion of a root that stores food. "Duck potato" is the edible tuber of Broad-leaved Arrowhead.

Index